The Maccabean Playbook

Then and Now

Moshe Pitchon

21stCenturyJudaism.com
Miami, Florida

cover: Ofra Ben-David

To Jeff Levis

My 97-year-old beautiful Jewish Greek cousin inspires me with his love for Israel and Jewish knowledge.

Miami, January 2025

Contents

Introduction

For hundreds of years, the Jews of antiquity lived under the rule of various empires, including the Babylonians, the Persians, the Hellenistic kingdoms of Egypt and Syria, the Romans, and their Christian successors. Throughout this long period, they seldom rebelled, even when provoked.

In this context of Yehud's subservience to great powers, the Maccabean revolt, the subsequent Hasmonean independent state, and the expansion of the Jewish nation beyond the narrow frontiers of Yehud were unique events in Jewish life.

That is, until the creation of the Third Jewish Commonwealth in the 20th century.

Historians explain the meaning of the Maccabean period, saying that" "after centuries of dependence on one empire after another, the Maccabean rising signified a renewal of Israel's active intervention in the development of its own history."[1]

Change the word "Maccabean" in the previous statement to "Zionism," and one could argue that two thousand years

---

[1] NOTH, MARTIN: *The History of Israel*, p. 383

later, the Jewish people face the same opportunities and challenges as the Hasmoneans did.

True, the "props" differ, but the scene, plot, and characters appear to be quite similar. It could be argued that this should not surprise anybody since it is widely known that history repeats itself.

This concept about history repeating itself was a prevalent belief in Greek mythology and those under the influence of the Hellenistic culture. The Biblical Ecclesiastes, probably composed during the Ptolemaic era in the third century B.C.E., shortly following Alexander's conquest, notably stated:

> *Only that shall happen.*
> *Which has happened,*
> *Only that occurs.*
> *Which has occurred;*
> *There is nothing new.*
> *Beneath the sun!*[2]

Voltaire, however, explained that this was a misconception. He said:

> "*History never repeats itself; man always does.*"

When taken to its logical conclusion, Jewish theology has to acknowledge that even God does not control the future because the future is heavily influenced by the actions of those living in the present.

---

[2] *Eccl.* 1: 9

If the people of the Third Jewish Commonwealth, the modern State of Israel, founded in 1948, repeat the same ideas and behaviors that led to the destruction of the Second Jewish Commonwealth, the Hasmonean kingdom, they will confirm George Santayana's dictum: "Those who cannot remember the past are condemned to repeat it."

The Hasmonean period lasted a hundred years. From the victory over the Seleucids in 164 B.C.E. to the Romans' entry into Jerusalem in 63 B.C.E.

The Hasmoneans, also known as the "Maccabees," were a rural priestly family led by Mattathias of the Joarib order, whose members rose to the position of High Priest and later declared themselves kings.

Their rise to prominence, which included the carving out of a vast territory encompassing the Galilee, Transjordan, Idumaea, [3] and much of the coastal plain, was the result of their reaction to the Seleucids' policies, whose empire included today's Syria and Lebanon, as well as parts of Israel, Iraq, and Turkey.

The "Maccabees" were the spiritual and ideological heirs of Nehemiah, the Jewish Persian governor who, almost three hundred years earlier, had inserted ritual ethnicity into politics.

The Jewish culture promoted by this priestly-warrior family was founded on a totalitarian structure based on the conviction that every aspect of life should be governed by

---

[3] The Edomites populated the land in and around the city of Hebron, known by its Greek name of Idumaea.

the mandates of a transcendent law as interpreted by their community.

Though tradition has maintained that the Maccabean revolt was solely a revolt against Hellenization, this is disingenuous.

The issue was not Hellenization in itself, as numerous aspects of Greek culture had already infiltrated the Jewish world, frequently going unnoticed as Greek in origin.

The Hasmoneans erected monuments, showcased stone slabs in their tombs, minted coins inspired by Greek designs, employed mercenaries, and adopted royal titles, in addition to adopting Greek names, attire, and Hellenistic symbols.

They exhibited the same behaviors as other contemporaneous monarchs, including hosting drinking parties, maintaining mistresses alongside their legitimate spouses, and persecuting relatives whom they suspected of having personal and political motives.

What the Maccabees drove out of Yehud was not Hellenism but polytheism. The Maccabees were able to reject Hellenistic gods while yet absorbing secular Hellenistic culture. [4]

---

[4] SAND, SHLOMO: *The Invention of the Jewish People*, pp. 156-157. FACKENHEIM, EMIL, L.: *Encounters Between Judaism and Modern Philosophy. A Preface to Future Jewish Thought*, p. 97

As Israeli philosopher Yeshayahu Leibowitz summed up, "The Hasmoneans war was aimed primarily against Jews and not against Greeks."[5]

The Hasmoneans' restoration of complete sovereignty did not unify the nation but rather exacerbated sectarian strife, eventually leading to a civil war.

The first victim of this revolt, in 167 B.C.E., was a Jew. The elderly priest Mattathias, "zealous for God,"[6] murdered a Jew who offered a sacrifice on a Greek altar at Modi'in.

Eventually, the Hasmoneans, like all totalitarian rulers, only knew "how to exploit religious hopes for political intrigues and how to amalgamate religious and political power."[7] Despite reclaiming the temple and terminating the persecution of Antiochus IV, Epiphanes, they continued their fighting. Their regime became corrupt and tyrannical. "Ultimately, the victory of the Hasmoneans led to the destruction of the Temple itself."[8]

The swift acquisition of territory, however, produced radical social changes in the population. The substantial increase of the officially "Jewish" population in Yehud resulted in an escalating division among previously harmonious groups. This demographic shift raised pressing questions about the "correct" way to be Jewish, contributing to an environment of growing factionalism.

---

[5] "Discourses of the Jewish Holidays"

[6] *1 Macc.* 2

[7] BUBER, MARTIN: "The Holy Way" in *On Judaism* [Nahum N. Glatzer ed.], p. 120

[8] BIALE, DAVID: *Power & Powerlessness in Jewish History*, p. 22

As a result, the fragile institutions of Jewish politics were further weakened, leaving a void in which extreme sects thrived. These sects, combined with the ongoing conflict between Jews and other ethnic groups in Yehud, eventually pushed the Second Temple state into a fatal confrontation with the Romans.

The Hasmonean kingdom was the final independent Jewish political and religious state until the formation of the Third Jewish Commonwealth—the State of Israel—nearly two millennia later.

Comparing these two independent states is, without a doubt, unavoidable. Ultimately, Judaism is the product of the accumulated experiences of the Jewish people. Understanding what has been learned, or should have been learned, and how those lessons are applied elucidates both the strengths and weaknesses of Judaism.

• • •

Modern technology has dramatically improved our lives. However, many of our habits are evolving as a result of this. One of them is reading long passages, not to mention books. In some ways, the lack of emphasis on reading recalls a time when orality dominated information.

The fluidity of oral presentations frequently prevents us from laying on a word or concept, leaving us more susceptible to the conclusions of others rather than our own.

I attempted to address the issue by using shorter paragraphs and writing what should have been three books in one. Those who are familiar with the Hasmonean story, which is the central and longest part of this book, can skip it if they so wish. The goal has not been to tell a story that has been told tens of times before, always using the same sources, Flavius Josephus and the Books of the Maccabees.

If I chose to tell it anyhow, it is because I think that the Second Jewish Commonwealth and the developing history of the Third Jewish Commonwealth can be viewed from a different angle from the perspective provided by the end of the twentieth century and the first quarter of the twenty-first century.

Since Judaism is the product of the Jewish people's cumulative experiences, comparing similar experiences—like creating an independent and sovereign state—should determine what the Jews have learned, or at the very least, serve as a warning.

From the Restoration to Alexander

Jerusalem's Fall 587 B.C.E.

> *"On the seventh day of the ninth month—that was
> the nineteenth year of King Nebuchadnezzar of
> Babylon—Nebuzaradan, the chief of the guards and
> officer of the king of Babylon, came to Jerusalem.
> He burned the House of the Lord, the king's palace,
> and all the houses of Jerusalem; he burned down
> the house of every notable person.*
> *The entire Chaldean force that was with the chief of
> the guard tore down the walls of Jerusalem on
> every side.*
> *The remnant of the people that was left in the city,
> the defectors who had gone over to the king of
> Babylon, and the remnant of the population were
> taken into exile by Nebuzaradan, the chief of the
> guards.*
> *But some of the poorest in the land were left by the
> chief of the guards to be vinedressers and field
> hands."*[9]

In the early sixth century B.C.E. [10]—on July 29th, 587 B.C.E.—
Jerusalem was invaded by the Babylonian Empire and a month
later systematically destroyed.

---

[9] *2 Kgs.* 26: 8-12.

[10] B.C.E. and C.E. = BCE stands for "Before the Common Era" (or Christian
Era). The word "common" simply means that it is based on the most frequently
used calendar system, the Gregorian Calendar.

Yehud's [11] ancient political and religious infrastructures, the monarchy, priesthood, scribalism, and prophecy, ceased to exist.

> Nebuchadnezzar *"carried into exile all of Jerusalem: all the officers and fighting men and all the craftsmen and artisans… Only the poorest people of the land were left."* [12]

Babylonian exiles certainly were put to forced labor, but there is no indication that they were reduced to slavery or treated inhumanly or prevented from continuing to develop their culture.

The nobility of Yehud were treated as befitting captives of their rank. Judean artisans and craftsmen were utilized on Nebuchadnezzar's great building projects in the capital, including the famous Hanging Gardens. They were not forced to assimilate and were able to stay together, settling beside Babylon itself in such southern Mesopotamian centers as Tel-Abib [13], Tel-Melah, Tel-Harsha, and Nippur. [14]

Levites, priests, and other former temple officials, unable to fulfill their designated roles, nonetheless established their own distinct groups. [15]

In addition to Babylonia, the TaNaKh indicates that many Judeans had also sought refuge in Egypt, while others had already departed for Moab, Ammon, and Edom.[16] The exiles,

---

[11] The name *Judea* is a Greek and Roman adaptation of the name *Yehuda* the name of the *Kingdom of Yehuda* (Judah). The use of the name *"Yehud"* through this book aims at maintaining a Jewish perspective of a territory that somehow varieted in length during the Persian, Greek and Hasmonean periods.

[12] *2 Kgs* 24: 10

[13] *Ezek.* 2: 59

[14] *Ezek.* 1: 3; *Ezek.* 3: 15; *Ezra* 2: 59= *Neh.* 7: 61; *Ezra* 8: 15-23

[15] *Ezra* 2: 36 ff.

[16] *Jer.* 40: 11

thus, were also expatriates that eventually decided to stay in the countries where they had gone after the catastrophe.

Alongside priests and prophets, elders took over functions of leadership, suggesting a fairly well-developed social, economic, and organizational substructure establishing the roots of what was to become one of the major areas of Jewish life for the next one thousand years.[17]

In their efforts to establish new lives, individuals also sought innovative religious explanations for the world around them. During this period, Babylonia emerged as a significant source of some of the most profound prophetic statements within the biblical tradition. Moreover, the era was marked by a remarkable cultic inventiveness that played a central role in laying the foundations for postbiblical Judaism.[18]

Certainly, this destruction and deportation was not a blessing in disguise. However, out of this tragedy, as out of all the tragedies kept in Israel's memory, a new and more powerful Jewish culture developed. The Egyptian community provided the Septuagint translation of the Hebrew Bible into Greek, while

---

[17] The Jewish community in Babylonia experienced significant growth and prosperity from the sixth century B.C.E. By the end of this period, approximately 500 years later, the population had expanded to over one million individuals.

[18] "From Babylonia during the [half century between the fall of Jerusalem to Nebuchadnezzar (in 587 B. C. E.) and the fall of Babylon to Cyrus (in 539 B. C. E.)] come some of the largest and most important bodies of Old Testament material: the prophecies of Ezekiel and 'Second Isaiah" (*Isa.* 40-55), the 'Holiness Code' (*Lev.* 17-26) and other elements of the 'Priestly' collection of traditions and laws which bulks larger in Genesis, Exodus, Leviticus, Numbers and probably Joshua, also a number of psalms and prophecies scattered as interpolations through the larger books, for example, *Isa.* 13f.- all these are commonly assigned to Babylonia. But it seems likely, besides, that much of the editorial work of the Deuteronomic school in the Pentateuch, Joshua, Judges, Samuel and Kings, was done there." SMITH, MORTON: *Palestinian Parties and Politics that Shaped the Old Testament*, pp. 75-76

their compatriots in Babylon were responsible for the Babylonian Talmud in the rabbinic period.

Still, the people from Yehud had been displaced, alienated from the place that gave them identity and security.

• • •

Not fifty years had gone by when an alliance of Persians and Medes, put together by Cyrus the Great, founder of the Achaemenid empire, conquered the Neo-Babylonian empire.

At the outset of his reign, Nabonidus, the last king of Babylon, faced military threats and internal discord. In an effort to address these pressing issues, he made the controversial decision to relocate the statues of all the patron deities from the principal cities of the empire to Babylon. While this action was intended to centralize religious authority and strengthen his rule, it inadvertently resulted in the demotion of Marduk, the chief god who epitomized the faith and identity of the city. This decision alienated the local population and incited the ire of the priests, who played a key role in the religious and social fabric of Babylonian society. Consequently, Nabonidus lost their vital support, further complicating his efforts to stabilize his reign.

Thus, when the disciplined Persian army crossed the Tigris River north of Babylonia, the city surrendered without resistance.

> *'Sippar was seized without battle. Nabonidus fled... And the army of Cyrus entered Babylon without battle.'* [19]

---

[19] ANET, p. 306

In a calculated move that skillfully intertwined religious respect, political strategy, and cultural sensitivity, in one of Cyrus' first actions to consolidate his power and facilitate a smooth transition of governance in Babylon, he returned the gods to their rightful temples. This decision was not merely symbolic; it reflected a profound understanding of the importance of religious practices that had been overlooked during the reign of Nabonidus.

By honoring these traditions and restoring both the temples and their deities, Cyrus's approach was designed to win the loyalty of the local populations and minimize potential resistance to Persian rule.

Having already returned the gods taken by Nabonidus to their original Babylonian cities, as well as to Assyria and Elam, and having rebuilt their ruined temples in the process, Cyrus now also ordered the restoration of the temple in Jerusalem. Since the Jews did not use images in their worship, he ordered instead the return of the temple vessels taken by Nebuchadnezzar.

From his palace at Ecbatana during his first regnal year, [20] Cyrus issued a decree:

> *"As for the house of God, which is at Jerusalem, let the house be built, the place where they offer fire sacrifice continually; its height shall be ninety feet and its breadth ninety feet, with three courses of great stones and one of timber. And let its cost be given from the king's house. Also let the gold and silver utensils of the house of God that were brought to Babylon be restored and brought again to the temple that is in Jerusalem, each to its place. And you shall put them in the house of God."* [21]

---

[20] 538 B.C.E.

[21] *Ezra* 6: 3-5

Those things that Nebuchadnezzar had taken from the temple in Jerusalem and were stored in Babylon [22] were handed over to Sheshbazaar, Yehud's newly appointed Persian governor. Sheshbazaar then traveled to Jerusalem, where he laid the foundations of what would be the "Second Temple."

The rebuilding of the Temple, however, would not occur immediately. It would be a fairly long process, taking approximately twenty-three years to complete.

While all the nations exiled from their lands by the Assyrians and Babylonians experienced displacement, only the Jews returned to their homeland to rebuild their ancestral temple. This return did not occur in a single wave; rather, it progressed through numerous phases over the course of at least a century.

Jerusalem was a devastated city; the whole province of Yehud was under miserable economic conditions due to the long years of political instability and a period of drought. [23]

The first generations of settlers who arrived with Sheshbazaar did not find the land unoccupied. Not all of the population of the kingdom of Israel had been exiled in 721 B.C.E. [24], nor had the entire Judean population been exiled in 586 B.C.E.

And, while the returnees held property rights, the remaining inhabitants actually occupied the land. Property claims made by the returnees against those who had stayed behind were contested in the courts. The non-exiled individuals asserted their ownership of the land and viewed the returnees as foreigners

---

[22] At Esaglia

[23] *Hag.* 1: 6, 9, 10 f.; *Hag.* 2: 16; *Zech.* 8: 10

[24] The kingdom of Israel was destroyed in 720 B.C.E. when the Neo-Assyrian empire captured Samaria the capital of the northern kingdom of Israel, and carried away many Israelites into captivity.

21

without legitimate rights to it, maintaining that the land rightfully belonged to them, the indigenous inhabitants.

The returnees had to confront the reality that, as members of the former upper class, they had been stripped of both their leadership positions and their property. [25]

In their efforts to re-establish their identity as a nation with the necessary hierarchies of power, the returnees claimed the status of Israel exclusively for themselves, treating those who had not been deported as foreigners. This resulted in a significant political dispute regarding dominance over the Temple construction project.

In addition to their economic and social claims, the returnees arrived with a clear religious agenda, one that has persisted throughout Jewish history: the creation of a self-segregated, ritually pure society inspired by the new temple and the vision of a new society outlined in the teachings of the prophet Ezekiel.

The returnees were equipped with a fanatical determination, strong leadership, and a paramilitary structure. They possessed an educated class, economic resources, and the support of the imperial court, which played a crucial role in the development and security of Jerusalem.

Most importantly, they kept close contact with those who stayed in Babylon. There was no push to empty the Diaspora, as a head tax was collected from every Diaspora community to support the Temple. Everyone derived benefits from the Temple's rituals— both those who participated actively and those who engaged vicariously through the celebration of holidays that paralleled Temple worship.

Spanning what are now Iran, Turkey, Egypt, and portions of Pakistan and Afghanistan, the Persian Empire was

---

[25] *Ezek.* 11: 15; *Ezek.* 33: 24

one of the largest empires in ancient history. It was governed by satrapies, each of which was further subdivided into smaller regions known as provinces. [26] Within this political and administrative framework, the little province of Yehud was a small, semi-autonomous Jewish region measuring just 25 miles long and 30 miles wide.

Sixteen years after the Cyrus decree and after the foundations of the Temple in Jerusalem were laid, Cyrus' successor, the Persian king Cambyses, died.[27] His death plunged the vast empire into a severe crisis, as various regions sought to reclaim their former independence.

It took nearly three years for Cambyses' successor, Darius I, to put down the rebellions. Once he succeeded, his position as the sole ruler was firmly established. However, the lessons learned from this turmoil were not overlooked.

In response to the uprisings and to promote loyalty while preventing further unrest, Darius I adopted a new strategy: relocating exiled communities and appointing compliant leaders to oversee the native population.

Thus, in 521 B.C.E., in the second year of Darius, a new wave of returning exiles departed from Babylon. This time, they were led by Zerubbabel—the remaining heir of 'David's house,' which had held the monarchy in Yehud since King David—and by Joshua, the High Priest of the Zadokite line, [28] representing the priesthood.

The Jews were divided. Those who aimed to organize a new community under civil leadership supported Zerubbabel. Many among them were looking to capitalize on the opportunities

---

[26] "Medinah," in Hebrew. The provinces, in turn, were subdivided into districts

[27] 522 B.C.E.

[28] Zadok was the first High Priest in the Temple built by Solomon

presented by the new Persian imperial policy. And there was also a group of lay leaders who had remained in Yehud during the exile who viewed the end of the Davidic monarchy as an opportunity to implement reforms that embodied their vision of a Judean society without a monarchy.

Those who were of the opinion that the new community should be organized on a religious basis maintained that Joshua, who came from a priestly family, should be the one to assume the leadership of the community.

Within this camp, there was also a group of priestly reformers who had been royal officials subject to the authority of the king and for whom the end of the monarchy made them independent for the first time. They certainly did not look for a restoration on the model of the pre-exilic monarchy.

During the Babylonian exile, these priestly reformers had already espoused the development of a cult administered solely by themselves. [29] It would have been difficult, if not impossible, for this group to carry out this projected reform under a restored Davidic monarchy, which they were now happy had ceased to exist.

Overall, while there was not outright opposition, there was a noticeable lack of support for reestablishing the monarchy. In practice, a separate kingdom was inherently incompatible with Persian imperial dominance. The Jews were allowed to reconstruct their homeland, but this did not mean the return of their kingdom.

Due to the Persian policy of denying political autonomy to smaller countries, Israel was not a vassal state but an integral component of the Persian Empire. Though the Jewish community of Yehud had some degree of autonomy, it was ultimately governed by the Persian administrative system.

---

[29] *Ezek.* 40-48

"The God of Heaven" had charged Cyrus and his successors with rebuilding the Temple of Jerusalem, not with reestablishing the Kingdom of David. [30]

In addition to this lack of consensus, there were theological objections from those who believed that the time to rebuild the temple had not yet arrived.

Despite this division, a broad coalition of interests ultimately facilitated the temple's reconstruction. The priesthood, for whom the rebuilding of the temple was essential for employment, livelihood, and the realization of their self-government plans, was naturally the most invested in the project.

Eventually, on the third day of the month of Adar in the sixth year of Darius's reign, in the spring of 515 B.C.E., the modest temple was dedicated. Israel had successfully established a cultic, literary, and theological center that also addressed the social dynamics within the community of Yehud. Once again, Israel had become a nation centered around a unifying focal point.

In time, however, the Temple, initially intended as a space that allowed Jews of all beliefs from Yehud and the Diaspora to cultivate a collective identity, would devolve into a stronghold of power. It would become a battleground for competing factions, a bank ripe for exploitation, and a military fortress that ultimately brought destruction to Jerusalem and its surrounding areas.

The house of David, already humiliated by having to share its power and priestly prerogatives with the house of Zadok, also had to contend with those Jews who believed that the misfortunes following the Temple's destruction by the Babylonians were entirely the fault of their kings, and as a result,

---

[30] BICKERMAN, ELIAS: *The Jews in the Greek Age*, p. 33

they opposed any descendant of this family from leading the people.

Zerubbabel capitulated, and the house of David vanished from Yehud as a political force.

The faction that supported Joshua ultimately triumphed. He became not only the High Priest in the rebuilt temple but also the sole leader in the new community. From the Restoration until the Hasmonean Revolt, [31] sole authority over the Jewish people would reside in the hands of Jerusalem's "Cohen Gadol." This position was acknowledged by foreign rulers, who held the High Priest accountable for maintaining order and collecting taxes. For the time being, it would be the Zadokite priests who set the religious and social agenda.

With both religious and political power concentrated in the High Priest's hands, Yehud functioned as a theocracy.

By the middle of the fifth century, rather than a kingdom, the small town of Jerusalem and the sparsely populated area of Yehud [32] had evolved into "a little flock with the makings of a church."

---

[31] 165 B.C.E.

[32] Charles Carter, *The Emergence of Yehud: A Social and Demographic Study* (1999), estimates that the population of the entire province of Yehud was only about 13,350 at the end of Babylonian period in the late sixth century B.C.E. Although this population would grow to about 20,650 by the end of the Persian rule in the mid-fourth century B.C.E. According to archaeologists, the city of Jerusalem itself never had a population of more than 1,500 during the Persian period.

"The list in *Ezra* 2 and *Neh.* 7 sets the number of returnees at 42,360 to which must be added 7,337 make and female slaves (*Ezra* 2: 64-65). The total of some twenty thousand persons deported [...] makes this number seem incredibly large, especially since it should probably be multiplied by a factor of three to allow for women and children. Even if we postulate a high birth rate, as is sometimes the case for ethnic minorities, and assume that exiles from earlier deportations joined the Babylonian golah, the number remains unrealistic, since we know from later returns (almost eight thousand more in

The priests of Joshua's lineage, the family of Zadok, ruled as High Priests, navigating the challenging years ahead and steadily expanding their power.

Following Darius I's death, once again, nationalistic efforts resurfaced across the Persian Empire.

Supported by 200 Athenian galleys stationed just fifty miles from Jerusalem, Egypt was in the midst of a major revolt. [33] As the Greek wars highlighted the fragility of Persian power, nationalistic forces in Yehud, aided by Egypt, were also striving to break free from Persian control.

If a significant inland city like Jerusalem were to revolt and ally with the Athenians, it could disrupt Persian lines of communication and potentially threaten their hold on Egypt. Therefore, the Persians were receptive to ideas that would pacify the local population, thereby ensuring their support.

After Artaxerxes I of Persia ascended to the throne, [34] a group of Babylonian Jews, consisting of the upper classes of Jerusalem exiled by Nebuchadnezzar, made two attempts to change religious practices in Jerusalem.

The leaders of these efforts were Nehemiah—one of several Jews serving in an administrative role within the Persian

---

Ezra 3: 1-30) and other sources that the majority of the Judean exiles stayed in Babylonia. It has therefore been suggested repeatedly that this list, as its position in *Neh.* 7 indicates, represents the total membership of the Judean community in the time of Nehemiah, all of whom had meanwhile come to think of themselves as descendant of the returnees. The number of those who returned through the year 520 probably does not exceed ten thousand."
ALBERTZ, RAINER: *Israel in Exile: The History and Literature of the Sixth Century B.C.E.*, pp. 127-128

[33] in 458 B.C.E.

[34] 464 B.C.E

imperial bureaucracy—and Ezra, a priest and descendant of Zadok.

These two men would eventually be regarded as the new commonwealth's founding fathers. Their decisions and actions would shape Judaism from the start of the Second Temple era and continue to do so to this day.

Their doctrine was founded on the belief that the catastrophes that the Assyrians, first, and the Babylonians later had inflicted upon Israel were the result of disloyalty to God, as foreshadowed by prophets such as Isaiah and Jeremiah.

They both sought to establish a pure community. They believed that only by transforming the remnant people into a theocratic nation—grounded in and faithful to the covenant made by God with their ancestors—could they revive the Davidic dynasty and anticipate resuming their mediatorial role among the nations of the earth.

Approximately 70 years after Zerubbabel completed the construction of the Temple, Nehemiah arranged for himself to be sent on an official mission to Jerusalem.

Because of his access to the king, Nehemiah, a descendant of the Babylonian exiles and a member of an ancient Jerusalemite family, had been lobbied by a delegation from Jerusalem led by his brother Hanani. The Jerusalemites were asking Nehemiah to request the king to repair the city's walls and gates; one hundred years after the Babylonians had destroyed them, they still remained in ruins.

In appointing, financing, and authorizing Nehemiah and later Ezra, the Persians were driven by practical considerations. Their actions were strategies to shore up the pro-Persian coalitions within their vast empire.

Beyond offering protection for the small community against harassment by neighboring peoples, the restoration of Jerusalem's walls held significant political importance for the Jews.

During the Persian Period, a city had to be a fortified town to attain the status of provincial capital. Although the temple had been rebuilt and Jerusalem had reestablished itself as the cultic center of the Judeans, its lack of fortifications prevented it from regaining its former status as Yehud's capital.

On the other hand, Samaria, the capital city of the former Kingdom of Israel, had long been transformed into an Assyrian province. The Neo-Babylonian and later Persian administrations had left this structure unchanged.

Because Yehud was ruled by a sub governor, the governor of the province of Samaria felt entitled to interfere in the affairs of Judah and Jerusalem, more or less at whim.

Nehemiah's construction bid would now separate Yehud from Samaria and raise it to the status of an independent province. As to be expected, this brought Nehemiah the enmity of Sanballat the governor of Samaria, whose plan had been to subjugate Yehud and, in time, to annex it.

The political tug-of-war between Nehemiah and Sanballat, however, was not the only conflict stirred by the newly appointed envoy.

He had also antagonized Yehud upper classes—among them, the influential land-owning Tobiads Jewish family [35] by compelling nobles and officials to take a solemn oath to stop charging the

---

[35] The Tobiads were an influential, land-owning Jewish family that had already established themselves across the Jordan in the old area of Ammon during the Judean monarchy and had gone into exile in Babylon with the rest of Jerusalem's aristocracy.

high interest that was forcing an impoverished and debt-ridden section of the population to sell their property and even sell their children and themselves as slaves to be able to pay their debts.

Tobiah's goals, along with those of Sanballat and other Persian officials, as well as local kings and nobles, were to undermine Nehemiah by, among other things, scaring the workers constructing the wall with threats of violence. [36]

Nehemiah, who had arrived in Jerusalem with a military escort of horsemen and their officers, [26] as part of his governmental appointment, was not easily intimidated. He rebuilt the walls in an impressively short period of time [28] preparing for the freshly fortified city to be closely guarded under a 'captain of the fortress' and issuing instructions to open the city gates in the morning and close them at night.

Paying little attention to the merchants' protestations, he also ordered the gates to close at sundown on Friday and not open until dusk on Saturday, in observance of the Shabbat.

Though Nehemiah was not a priest but a layman, his goal had been to implement a religious ideology in the political realm, which encompassed the exclusion of foreign influences, intermarriage, and the integrity and purity of the temple and its personnel.[37]

It had taken some 70 years between the fall of Jerusalem and the completion of the second temple, and another 70 years between the temple's completion and Nehemiah's arrival in the province, as well as the completion of Jerusalem's wall.

---

[36] *Neh.* 4: 7-8
[37] BLENKINSOPP, JOSEPH: *Judaism: The First Phase*, p. 230

In the year 458 B.C.E., King Artaxerxes I of Persia appointed Ezra special royal commissioner for Judean affairs and sent him to Jerusalem on behalf of the Persian crown.

By descent a priest and by profession a scribe, Ezra arrived in Jerusalem with 2,000 men, women, and children, *"all those who tremble (Haredim) at the words of the God of Israel."* [38] He also brought with him the Torah of Moses—"Judaism's Magna Carta."

Though a descendant of Zadok, but not himself a High Priest, Ezra had been empowered by the Persian monarch with the same prerogatives as all High Priests in Israel, namely to appoint judges and punish those who violated the laws of God and the king through death, confiscation, or imprisonment.

The High Priest's supremacy essentially represented the reimposition of the authority of the old ruling classes upon groups who had remained in the land and who had opposed the returnees.

Yehud was now officially a theocracy, or more appropriately a nomocracy [39] since even the High Priest- who had sole authority over the Jewish people—was limited by the laws in the Torah. "Unable to crown a king, the exiles canonized a set of texts." [40]

The Jerusalem High Priest office was hereditary, restricted to the Zadokite line of the priesthood. Still, it was the imperial ruler who approved or disapproved who would occupy the post. The High Priest, who was thus both an imperial official and a representative of the Jewish people, was in charge of all cultic matters at the Temple, as well as all civil issues, order

---

[38] *Ez.9: 4*

[39] A government in accordance with a system of law

[40] WALZER, MICHAEL: *In God's Shadow: Politics in the Hebrew Bible* (Kindle loc. 2039)

preservation, and the collection and delivery of taxes to the empire.

Ezra's title was *Sofer Data*, intended to mean a "Scribe" or "Secretary" for Jewish Law. [41] He brought to Jerusalem a collection of the Jewish people's ancestral laws that had been gathered together by the *soferim*, the scribe class, during the Exile. This law collection had been in force before 539 B.C.E., when the Cyrus edict restoring the Jews right to come back to their land and rebuild their homeland was enacted. Thus, the Torah became the final law of Israel.

Artaxerxes had made Moses' word the king's law in respect to the royal administration of the Jews."In the century that separated Nehemiah from Alexander, and again during the 160 years from Alexander to Antiochus Epiphanes, eight generations of Jews were brought up under the discipline of the Torah, a discipline under which dissidents were seen both as heretics and as rebels." [42]

Together with bringing the Law, Ezra and his fellow *Haredim* had a deliberate agenda of establishing a ritually pure community by introducing the novel argument that all of Israel—not just the priestly class—constitutes a holy seed distinct from the profane seed of Gentiles. Accordingly, genealogical purity was required of all Israelites to protect against the 'profanation' of the sacred seed. This has been a defining aspect of Israel's religious system throughout the centuries and a central factor in the internal battles dividing Jews.

---

[41] Interestingly, the Persian word for law, "*dat*," in Hebrew came to mean "religion." In today's Israel, people living according to the tenets of Jewish religious law are called "*datim*," that is, they live according to religious Jewish law.

[42] BICKERMAN, ELIAS: *The Jews in the Greek Age*, p. 31

The Ptolemies and Seleucids Conflict

The Persian Empire, founded by Cyrus the Great, ruled over dozens of different nations, at its zenith accounting for 44% of the ancient world population. However, it had ruled for nearly two centuries [43] on a shaky foundation.

Not only did the population they ruled outnumber the Persians several times over, but the empire lacked a solid internal authority and proper means of self-defense, all of which made the Achaemenids highly vulnerable.

So, when on November 5, 333 B.C.E., Alexander of Macedon, leading a Greek army, defeated Darius III of Persia and his hosts at Issus, the historic gateway from Asia Minor to Syria and Egypt lay wide open.

Four days after the victory, Alexander's cavalry crossed over the passes of Mount Amanus and entered Damascus, the capital of the Persian satrapy of Syria. Alexander himself moved down the coast of Tyre, Gaza, and on into Egypt.

Alexander's decade of Eastern conquests enabled the combination of Western and Eastern cultures, a merging of cultures that continued uninterrupted for subsequent centuries after his death.[44]

---

[43] From 559 B.C.E. to 330 B.C.E.

[44] "The conquest of Persia by Alexander the Great inaugurated the *Hellenistic period*." COHEN, D., SHAYE: *From the Maccabees to the Mishnah*, p. 2

The transition from Persian to Greek rule went smoothly; Alexander took over the Persian system of administration and followed the same policy of religious tolerance. So, in Jerusalem, nothing changed with Alexander's arrival other than the name of the pagan sovereign. The rulers of the people, the tribute, and the status of the Temple all remained as they had been under the Persian monarchs.

Alexander died of fever at Babylon on the evening of June 10, 323 B.C.E. With no clear successor, his generals [45] fought over his empire.

In 316 B.C.E., Antigonus, who had been satrap of Phrygia in Asia Minor while Alexander was alive, extended his control not only over all of Asia Minor but also over Syria, Mesopotamia, Persia, and Media. Considering himself the supreme ruler of all of Alexander's heritage, he demanded that others yield completely to his power.

Four years later, Ptolemy I—Alexander's general, who had inherited control of Egypt—seized an opportunity when Antigonus was engaged in warfare outside Syria and the country had been left under the management of his young son Demetrius to invade Coele Syria. [46] Helped by Seleucus I, his one-time comrade-in-arms Ptolemy I met Demetrius near Gaza. The fight was long and obstinate, but Ptolemy I and Seleucus I were ultimately victorious, and Demetrius abandoned the field and fled northward. The whole of Coele Syria, as far as the Phoenician cities were concerned, fell into Ptolemy's hands.

---

[45] The *diadochi*, or 'Successors,' was how to the Macedonian generals who succeeded Alexander were known through history.

[46] The area that encompassed the provinces of Syria and Phoenicia and it was one of the few entry points into Egypt

In 302 B.C.E., the Macedonian generals, who by that time had turned themselves into kings, leagued together for a joint war against Antigonus.

Lysimachus, the monarch of Thrace, aided by Cassander, king of Macedon's expeditionary force, invaded Asia Minor, forcing Antigonus to summon his son, Demetrius, and his army from Greece.

The decisive battle between the army of Antigonus and Demetrius and the joint army of Lysimachus, Cassander, and Seleucus took place at Ipsus in Phrygia in 301 B.C.E. Antigonus was killed and his army defeated.

According to the rules of war, the victors were entitled to the defeated enemy's possessions, and Lysimachus and Cassander, Seleucus' partners in the victory at Ipsus, had agreed to give him control over the Syrian satrapy.

Ptolemy I, who had been absent from the battlefield, however, demanded Syria and Phoenicia upon the 'spear-won land' principle. Because he and not Seleucus I, was the occupying king, he claimed the southern part of the Syrian satrapy for himself.

The Syrian satrapy was now *de facto* divided. Seleucus held its northern part, while Ptolemy held the southern section, which included Yehud.

Initially, due to Ptolemy I's prior assistance to the founder of the Seleucid empire, Seleucus I refrained from asserting his claim, but his successors maintained their belief that the region rightly belonged to them. The outcome was a succession of conflicts known as the "Syrian wars," during which the Seleucids endeavored to reclaim the territory.

Because the land of Israel lies at the point where Africa, Asia, and Europe meet it constitutes the only land bridge for the mighty kingdoms on both sides of the Fertile Crescent, and thus it has occupied, then as today, a central place in the geopolitical framework of the Near East.

Anyone wishing to invade Egypt had to pass through the Phoenician coast. The land of Yehud was near the military route of Egypt, not far from the final halting places on Asiatic soil before the passage through the Sinaitic deserts into the land of the Nile. During the Hellenistic age, between 323 and 30 B.C.E., Jerusalem would thus be ground zero for more than twenty conflicts.

Five times in the course of the third century B.C.E. alone— the kings of the South and the kings of the North, as the biblical book of *Daniel* calls them—the Ptolemies of Alexandria and the Seleucids of Antioch went to war.

Yehud, finding itself now located at the boundary of the two opposing dynasties, had its citizens divided into two factions, each loyal to one of the contending superpowers. The conflict shifted from a confrontation between the Holy City and the pagan authority to an internal discord among factions of two competing pagan kingdoms. The victor of one of the factions penalized the other.

After the turbulent phase of the wars of the Diadochi, [47]in which the Jewish population of Yehud, too, had

---

[47] 321-301 B.C.E.

experienced all the harshness of the superior Macedonian war machine. Yehud fell into the hands of Ptolemy I. [48]

Although Egypt was a rich country, attractive to foreign settlers, the Ptolemaic province of Syria and Phoenicia was important for the Egyptian economy. To the Ptolemies, the region was just another milk cow, providing goods and revenues.[49]

Though the Ptolemies granted Yehud a partially autonomous status—'to live in accordance with ancestral laws'—Yehud, as the rest of Coele Syria, was governed as another province of Egypt; it was administered from Alexandria with Egyptian agents in the various cities and villages to see that the appropriate taxes were paid and the Ptolemaic interests served.

Under the Ptolemies, the right to collect the taxes for each city was auctioned each year in Alexandria and was usually bought either by the leaders of the city or by its leading citizens.

In 240 B.C.E., Onias II, the High Priest of Jerusalem, had been reluctant to pay the tribute to Egypt. Onias II was pro-Seleucid and was hoping for a change of political fortune that would render the payment to Egypt unnecessary.

---

[48] Ptolemy I ruled Egypt since 305 B.C.E. and had the Alexandrian Library built. It was during his reign or his son, Ptolemy II the Great that the Torah was translated into Greek.

[49] The variety of agricultural products exported to Egypt was large, the main ones being wheat, wine, and oil. Another important product from Egypt's point of view was slaves, both for employment in the households of nobles and to work in the wool trade.

The king, angered, sent his envoy to Jerusalem with a severe message and the threat that, if Onias did not pay, he would divide the Jewish territory and would settle military troops in Jerusalem.

Despite the threats, Onias refused to yield and stood his ground. He declared that he would rather surrender the high priesthood, if necessary, than pay the tribute.

Onias II's nephew, Joseph, the son of Onias II's sister and Tobiah—a descendant of Tobiah the Ammonite, who had clashed with Nehemiah some 200 years earlier—on learning that Ptolemy's representatives were about to seize the country, declared himself ready to take personal responsibility for the payment of the tribute due to Egypt.

Though Joseph was a nephew of the High Priest on the maternal side and he, himself a priest, he could not take the office of the High Priest, which was hereditary and could only go to the oldest son.
Civil leadership, however, could be transmitted without facing the problem of hereditary succession. Thus, the decision was made to separate the two functions, with Onias transmitting the civil leadership to his nephew Joseph.

When the High Priest was relieved of the responsibility for the levying of taxes and their transmission to the Ptolemaic monarch, the initial breach in Jerusalem's theocracy occurred. The task was now in the hands of a professional financier.

Joseph ben Tobiah convoked an assembly of the people in the Temple and proposed himself as emissary to the king to effect a compromise in the dispute. Once the people had agreed to his proposal, Joseph called on the envoy of King Ptolemy. He entertained him for several days and presented him with expensive gifts. Won over by his generosity and impressed by his dignity, the Egyptian envoy encouraged Joseph to proceed to the king, promising to help him obtain assent to his requests.

After having borrowed money for the journey from friends in Samaria, Joseph ben Tobiah went down to Egypt to appear there before the king as chief of the Jews.

Flavius Josephus gives us a vivid account of the lobbying, graft, and corruption that went on in the Ptolemaic court in connection with the tax auction. [50] Being familiar with the court through his father's commercial relations, as well as his own, Joseph ben Tobiah accused the native tax-collector bidders of collusion and promised to pay a much greater amount into the royal treasury than it had thus far received.

Joseph succeeded not only in softening the king's wrath but also in negotiating a successful deal in his own favor. He was awarded the contract to collect the taxes not only in Yehud but in all of Ptolemaic Coele-Syria.

Tax collection having never been popular, Joseph was empowered to use royal troops if he met with resistance; therefore, Ptolemy assigned 2,000 soldiers to help Joseph. In fact, when Joseph came to the city of Ascalon to collect the taxes, he met with resistance. He arrested twenty leaders of the recalcitrants, executed them, confiscated

---

[50] *Ant.* 12.4.2 (167-179

their property, and turned it over to the king. He repeated
the same measures when he came to Scythopolis. Though
the king commended him for his bravery, Joseph's stern
treatment created ill will between the Greeks and the
Judaeans. [51] The Coele-Syrians looked upon him as a
Judaean who had usurped power to oppress them.

When Zenon, a Ptolemaic officer, visited Judah on an
official mission, he ignored the Jerusalem priesthood and
dispatched all his business outside Jerusalem with Joseph,
who was manifestly the one in charge of the political,
economic, and military affairs of the region on behalf of
the Ptolemies.

In a single stroke, ben Tobiah had deposed the local
aristocracy and achieved for himself, in practice, if not in
law, a status unrivaled in the entire province. He remained
the general contractor for the taxes of Ptolemaic Syria for
twenty-two years, becoming one of the richest men of his
generation.

The trajectory of the Tobiad family, whose influence in
Jewish society Nehemiah and Ezra struggled to minimize,
had just been reinvigorated with him.

Through this powerful family, Jerusalem acquired new
importance by becoming the seat of the head tax collector.
Many of the sub-collectors and principal men of Coele-
Syria had to travel to Jerusalem on official business, and
some took up residence there. Many of the inhabitants now
began to speak Greek. Gradually the lives of the Judeans
underwent a significant change. From an obscure small

---

[51] *Ant.* 12. 4. 2 (167- 179

city, Jerusalem became one of the most important cities in Coele-Syria, simultaneously improving the Judeans economic conditions.

. . .

In 217 B.C.E., four years after taking the throne, Antiochus III of Syria embarked on a campaign against the Egyptian Ptolemaic monarchy. The Ptolemaic army, which included a Greek phalanx unit of 25,000 soldiers and an Egyptian phalanx unit of 20,000 soldiers, was the largest of the two contenders, enabling Ptolemy IV Philopator to come out victorious over Antiochus III forces.

The historian Polybius emphasizes that after the victory, different cities competed with one another in expressing their loyalty to the Ptolemaic king. Jerusalem was among those who enthusiastically welcomed Ptolemy IV Philopator.

Antiochus III, never one to give up, waited sixteen years before attempting to recapture Coele-Syria from the Ptolemies.

In 204, Ptolemy IV Philopator died, and Ptolemy V Epiphanes, a child of five, ascended the throne. The power passed to the king's guardians, and when their rule was unsuccessful, there began a growing popular ferment among the Egyptians, especially among the citizens of Alexandria. Antiochus III jumped at the opportunity presented by these disturbances to finally carry out his conquering designs.

So, three years later, Antiochus III launched the Fifth Syrian War by invading Syria and Phoenicia. The inhabitants of Coele- Syria showed little or no resistance to the advancing Seleucid army; perhaps they even supported Antiochus III. Thanks to this kind of behavior, the Seleucids were able to invade Syria and Phoenicia very quickly.

Though Antiochus III had occupied Jerusalem, an Egyptian general by the name of Scopas reconquered the city in the winter of 201-202 B.C.E.

Scopas had met with resistance from the Jews, who helped the Seleucid army take control of the citadel in Jerusalem where the Ptolemaic garrison was encamped. He punished the heads of the pro-Seleucid faction and stationed a strong garrison in the citadel of Zion, northwest of the Temple. Antiochus III took back the city later in 200 B.C.E., after a long siege that left Jerusalem in ruins.

In recovering Jerusalem, Antiochus III had been aided by the city's traditional aristocracy and by the High Priest, Simon II, a Zadokite who stood at the head of the pro-Seleucid party. He demonstrated his gratitude to his supporters by relieving the secular aristocracy and the priestly caste of personal taxes.

Caught between Syria and Egypt, Jerusalem had been once again, as in the days of Isaiah and Jeremiah, torn apart by opposing factions, one favoring Antiochus, the other inclining to Ptolemy.

Thanks to their relation with the Tobiads, by the time the Seleucids took over from the Ptolemies, the Jerusalem priesthood had become a political and economic power that could no longer be ignored by the king. Antiochus III restored the High Priest, Simon II, known as "the Righteous One" [52], to his position as head of the nation and once again delegated to him the responsibility for the collection of the tribute. Simon also undertook the task of rebuilding the town and the Temple. Flowing water was conducted into the city, and the wall was rebuilt.

Many Jews, however, had expected that the change from the Ptolemaic regime to the Seleucid would be less burdensome. The reality, however, had been different. Antiochus III, under whose rule they had now passed, engaged in costly wars, none costlier than his war with Rome, which both reduced the extent of his kingdom and involved him in the payment of a large indemnity to Rome, spread over a number of years. He was therefore compelled to impose heavier taxation on his subjects than the Ptolemies had imposed.

Antiochus III died in the course of an attack on the temple at Elymais near Susa. He left two sons: Antiochus, who was in Rome as a hostage, and Seleucus, who ascended the throne as Seleucus IV Philopator.

During the reign of Seleucus IV Philopator, Onias III became High Priest in Jerusalem.

This son of the High Priest Simon II did not seem to be as capable of asserting himself in the political, economic, and religious complexities as his father was. The high priestly families within Jerusalem were at loggerheads with one

---

[52] *hassaddiq*

another, and Onias III had to fight to avoid being deposed by one of them.

The Temple's treasury was increasingly becoming the private fund of a few highly placed families that wielded power in the city. The sons of Tobias among them, controlling the state through their supervision of the market, collection of taxes, and exercise of other financial privileges.

A sharp struggle emerged between the High Priest Onias III and his cousin Simon of Bilgah, the head of the temple administration and a supporter of the Tobiads. Simon sought the additional role of administrator of the city market. When Onias III refused to consolidate these two important offices in one individual, Simon conspired against him with Apollonious, the Seleucid governor.

Simon of Bilgah accused the High Priest of forming an alliance with another of the Tobiads, Hyrcanus Tobiah, who favored the Ptolemies and was an adversary of the Seleucids, by permitting him to deposit his funds in the Temple. To support his accusation, he argued that if the daily sacrifices were financed from the Seleucid treasury, then why had the Temple accumulated an unusual surplus?

Seleucus IV sent his chief minister, Heliodorus, to investigate the charges.

When Heliodorus arrived in Jerusalem, he was warmly received by Onias III. However, when Seleucus's chief minister expressed his desire to enter the Temple to confiscate the money believed to be hidden there, he was denied access. Onias explained that much of the money had been deposited by widows and orphans. While he acknowledged that some of the funds in the Temple belonged to Hyrcanus, he defended him against accusations made by his adversary, his half-brother Simon of Bilgah. Onias further stated to Heliodorus that it would be both wrong and sacrilegious to enter the Temple and seize the money entrusted to its sanctity by the faithful.

It seems that Heliodorus came into some sort of arrangement with Onias III, enabling them to settle the matter satisfactorily. Heliodorus already had formed plans to assassinate his king, Seleucus IV, and crown himself King of Syria. Perhaps he thought it advisable to have the high priest of the Temple of Jerusalem and the leader of the Judeans as his friend.

In 175 B.C.E., Heliodorus effectively murdered Seleucus IV. Bypassing his eldest son, Demetrius—who was serving as a hostage in Rome in place of his uncle Antiochus— Heliodorus appointed himself regent for Seleucus IV's youngest son. His intention was clear: to use the child as a façade for his own ambitions and to secure effective control over the kingdom.

Onias III, fearing the possibility of civil war in Jerusalem in which Simon of Bilgah and the sons of Joseph Tobiah would have the protection of Apollonius, the governor of Coele-Syria, set out for Antioch to see King Seleucus in person. Seleucus IV, however, was in the meantime murdered.

Antiochus, the brother of the assassinated Seleucus IV, successfully rallied enough support from the Greek ruling class in Antioch to claim the throne. He argued that the legitimate successor, Seleucus IV's eldest son, Demetrius, was still very young and a hostage in Rome.

Outmaneuvering Heliodorus, Antiochus adopted the name Antiochus IV Epiphanes and proclaimed himself co-regent with his brother's youngest infant son, also named Antiochus.[53]

Onias III remained in Antioch for some time after Antiochus IV Epiphanes ascended the throne. The new king, however, was ill-disposed to him. Onias III suspected him of being too friendly to the Ptolemies; Coele-Syria had only been wrested from Ptolemaic hands recently, and Antiochus IV Epiphanes thus wanted to dismiss officials who might welcome the Ptolemies back too eagerly.

Realizing that the new king was unfavorably disposed to him and that, apparently, there was a plot against his life, Onias III fled to Egypt, where he later received permission from Ptolemy and Cleopatra to build a temple in Heliopolis, which became known as the House of Onias.[54]

With the High Priest post in Jerusalem vacant, Onias III's brother, Jason (Joshua), applied to Antiochus IV Epiphanes to confirm him in the position, promising to pay the large sum of 360 talents (probably the regular tribute) plus another 80 talents. In addition, he paid 150 talents to have Jerusalem made into a Greek foundation with a gymnasium

---

[53] Antiochus, son of Seleucus IV would later die in 170 BC, possibly murdered by Antiochus IV

[54] The year 168 B.C.E. was the most suitable for building a temple in Egypt, for in that very year the Temple in Jerusalem was defiled by Antiochus IV, Epiphanes.

and *ephebeion* [55] and the prerogative of drawing up a list of people to be citizens of a *polis* within Jerusalem to be called Antiochenes in honor of the King.

Antiochus IV Epiphanes, haunted by his father's defeat, believed that conquering the Eastern Mediterranean coast was critical in the long run. He had concluded that the eastern states' disunity was one of the primary causes of the Roman victory.

Determined to prevent a recurrence of this scenario, Epiphanes main concern was to prevent Roman penetration into the Near East. He thus aimed at uniting Syria and Egypt into a single state under Seleucid rule. He began a project to Hellenize all his eastern territories to create a homogeneous state governed by a strong central authority.

The small country of Yehud thus became very important to Antiochus because she could serve as a base for his proposed attack on Egypt.

To secure the complete loyalty of Yehud, he had to rely upon the sons of Joseph, who now were pro-Seleucid and favored Yehud's Hellenization.

The Tobias family had been responsible for converting Jerusalem from an obscure, insignificant town into a prominent city. But their economic gains could only be fulfilled if Jerusalem could have the privileges of a Hellenistic city. They felt handicapped in their commercial enterprises because Jerusalem did not have the privilege of coinage, whereas other cities, like Tyre, did. They knew

---

[55] institute for Greek education

they could not have achieved their goal as long as Onias III was the high priest and thus supported Jason.

So, Jason, exploiting at once his own position and the royal bankruptcy, got himself confirmed in the position. This was in itself a violent departure from Jewish tradition since only the eldest son, not a brother, could succeed his father in that office while a son was still living.

Jason clearly thought of himself as a full and faithful Jew, even though he got permission for Jerusalem to become a Greek foundation. Being "Hellenized" did not mean losing one's Jewish identity. Judaism and Hellenism were neither competing systems nor incompatible concepts. It would be incorrect to assume that Hellenization resulted in the erosion of Jewish traditions and beliefs. Jews did not have to choose between assimilation or resistance to Greek culture.

Despite the fact that it has frequently been simplified as a conflict between "Hellenizers" and a true-to-Yehud party. In reality, the conflict between the parties was primarily about family avarice and dynastic lust within the Temple administration.

The fact remains that members of Jerusalem's religious establishment found it perfectly acceptable to participate in the gymnasium's activities while maintaining their sacerdotal role.

The Romans and Jews were the only people in antiquity who accepted Hellenistic civilization. The others remained averse to it. The Jews alone among all the Orientals were able to accept Hellenic civilization and also preserve their individuality. [56]

Three years after his appointment, Jason sent a priest named Menelaus to Antiochus with the promised money to the Seleucid king. Menelaus capitalized on the opportunity to nab the High Priest's position by offering Antiochus a sum of money that surpassed the 300 talents Jason had paid for his position. In addition to being captivated by the financial offer, Antiochus IV Epiphanes also sympathized with Menelaus' assurance of increased fervor in Hellenization.

Menelaus was appointed as the high priest by the king, who dismissed Jason.

> *"This was a monstrous intervention of the royal power in an internal concern of the religious community of Jerusalem, but it was not due to the king's own initiative. It was brought about by certain circles of the Jerusalem priesthood itself, which tried to obtain the king's support in their struggle for power, thereby inciting the king to intervene now and in the future in the appointment of the high priest and in the religious affairs of Jerusalem in general."* [57]

---

[56] For instance, post-Maccabean Judaism adopted the most important idea of Hellenism, that of perfection through liberal education. The Pharisees regarded universal instruction as basic to Judaism. They established a school in every village in the land of Israel. BICKERMAN, ELIAS, J: "The Historical Foundations of Postbiblical Judaism," in *The Jews: Their History, Culture and Religion*, Louis Finkelstein (ed.), Vol. I, p. 110

[57] NOTH, MARTIN: *The History of Israel*, p. 363

Jason did not yield his place without attempting to defend it, but an officer named Sostrates was sent by Antiochus with a troop of Cyprian soldiers to subdue any opposition that might be attempted by the followers of the now deposed high priest Jason and to collect at the same time the sum Menelaus had promised.

A civil war broke out in Jerusalem with the Tobiads on Menelaus's side. Jason fled the country to Jordan.

Due to King Antiochus's military support, Menelaus was able to become a High Priest. He employed royal edicts and military force to compel the Jews of Yehud and Jerusalem to obedience, in the same manner as Ezra and Nehemiah had imposed their views through the authority of the Persian kings in the past.

The failures of the High Priesthood as an institution became evident as the qualifying requirements for the position became increasingly compromised. The role was effectively auctioned to the highest bidder, someone with political affiliations to the foreign rulers who not only appointed these individuals but could also dismiss them as interests shifted.

Menelaus had promised Antiochus IV, Epiphanes, King of Syria, a large sum of money in a short time, but he found that the Temple treasury did not contain enough to pay the sum he had promised. He then traveled to Syria to excuse himself before the king and win some time. All the while leaving his brother Lysimachus to replace him as high priest during his absence and go about raising the necessary funds.

Lysimachus proceeded to rob the Temple of many golden vessels, a sacrilegious act that incited great indignation among the people. The spoliation of the Temple's treasures was difficult to conceal from the community. These treasures, accumulated over generations, belonged to all of Israel, and it was inexcusable for a small group to dispose of them as if they were their own.

Onias III, living in exile in Antioch, publicly denounced Menelaus for stealing sacred gold vessels from the Temple.

Menelaus, in turn, bribed Andronicus, the temporary governor of Antioch, to assassinate Onias III, the last legitimate Zadokite High Priest.

The Hasidic followers of Onias III were most plausibly the instigators of the temple riots. These Hasidim were religious extremists who arose in response to other extremists who, in their opinion, were willing to abandon Judaism for Hellenism. They belonged to the scribes who had gathered around Ezra and Nehemiah over two centuries earlier.

Crowds rioted in Jerusalem, and Lysimachus, with around 300 armed men, led a battle in the streets. Although many Judaeans were killed, the people ultimately emerged victorious: Lysimachus's men retreated, and he himself was killed near the Temple.

Subsequently, three men, representatives of the *gerousia* [58], the Temple Council, made up of citizens of the new Hellenistic aristocracy of Jerusalem set up by Jason,

---

[58] The Temple Senate, also known as the ruling council or the precursor of the Sanhedrin

appeared before the king to present charges against Menelaus.

Menelaus not only cleared himself of the charges by bribing Ptolemy, the son of Dorymenes, a friend of the king, but also gained further favor with Antiochus Epiphanes.

He accused the people of Jerusalem of being Egyptian supporters and claimed that they persecuted him solely because he opposed their political intrigues. This accusation led to the execution of the three deputies of the gerousia, even though they had proven beyond any doubt that Menelaus and Lysimachus had desecrated the Temple. When three more opponents of Menelaus denounced him at Tyre, Menelaus bribed the judge to also execute them.

Many prominent Hasidim priests left Jerusalem at this time, both for their own safety and because they chose not to continue serving in a temple run by their leader's murderers. By 166 B.C.E., the Hasidim were living in exile from Jerusalem, boycotting the temple, and achieving a reputation for their militant opposition to the Hellenists.

In the midst of all the turmoil in Yehud, in November 170 B.C.E., the Egyptian Ptolemaic army was moving out of the town of Pelusium to begin its invasion of Coele-Syria. Antiochus responded with a counterattack, which soon turned into an invasion of Egypt itself. He advanced into Egypt proper, conquering all but Alexandria. Egypt, now divided between two rival kings, was at Epiphanes's mercy.

This achievement was partially made possible because Rome—Ptolemaic Egypt's traditional ally—was embroiled in the Third Macedonian War and was not willing to become involved elsewhere. For Antiochus IV, Epiphanes, this was a great success. It was the first time since Alexander the Great that Egypt was successfully invaded from Coele-Syria, something that had evaded his father, Antiochus III, the Great.

During the years 169–168 B.C.E., Antiochus led a large army on another attack against Egypt. This time he had every chance of a complete victory.

After three wars against Macedonian kings, the Romans decided it was time to end the centuries-old Macedonian monarchy by dividing the kingdom into four separate states, each of which was free but required to pay tribute to Rome.

With firm control over the eastern Mediterranean coast, the Roman Senate saw Antiochus IV Epiphanes' proposed annexation of Egypt as a threat to their country.

The consul Popilius Laenas led an embassy to Antiochus, demanding that Antiochus IV retire from Egypt.

When Antiochus requested time to seek counsel, Popilius Laeanas issued a stern ultimatum. He drew a circle around Antiochus and instructed him to "decide on the spot and not leave that ring until he had given an answer to the Senate whether he would have peace or war with Rome." Antiochus replied that he would obey the Senate.

Compelled by Rome's order to withdraw completely from Egypt, he returned along the Phoenician coast, "groaning and bitter in heart," according to one ancient historian.

While Antiochus was at war with Egypt in 168 B.C.E., wishful thinking most likely fueled the spread of false rumors about the king's death, and as a result, Jason, who had been deposed as High Priest three years earlier and forced to flee to Transjordan, returned to Jerusalem and attempted to reestablish his rule.

Jason, leading a small force of about a thousand men, surprised Jerusalem. He took control of the city and temporarily forced the Seleucid High Priest Menelaus to seek refuge.

The atmosphere in Jerusalem, which had been tense even before Antiochus IV ascended the throne, erupted into a second civil war, with bloody riots breaking out in the streets.

According to Josephus, [59] this revolt was primarily a power struggle between the pro-Egyptian party, which sided with Jason, and the sons of Joseph, the Tobias family, and their supporters, who sided with the Seleucid High Priest Menalaus.

Jason failed in his attempt to retake his old position because he had to fight both Menelaus' followers and those of his own brother Onias. He also did not receive enough public support to take control of the city. He was forced to

---

[59] *War I 31- 3; Ant.* XII 239-41

flee once more to the land east of the Jordan, where he had retired following his first deposition.

The news of Jason's siege of Menelaus most likely reached Antiochus IV when the Romans forced him to leave Egypt.

At the same time, a dissident movement arose in the Phoenician city of Arad. Antiochus realized that he could not afford unrest and potential civil war in Yehud. The city served as a buffer country, protecting him in the event of an Egyptian attack.

The uprising had been a demonstration of hostility toward Syria since Menelaus was now the accredited puppet of Antiochus Epiphanes. The Syrian was thus forced to intervene to protect his control of Yehud. He had to put down the Jewish uprising with a strong hand.

In the autumn of 168 B.C.E., Epiphanes dispatched a force led by Apollonios, a regimental commander, to put down what he saw as a rebellion against him.

Apollonios marched against Jerusalem with a force of 22,000 men. He carried out a three-day massacre that killed both young and old, as well as women and children. In total, eighty thousand people were lost, forty thousand meeting violent deaths and an equal number being sold into slavery. Many survivors sought refuge by hiding or fleeing the city.

The wars with Egypt had drained Epiphanes' treasury, and he needed money more than ever. As a result, he stripped the Temple of its gold and silver vessels, as well as the golden altar, menorah, display table, and sacred curtains.

Apollonius constructed a stronghold known as the Akra in the City of David, south of the Temple Mount, after tearing down the city's walls. This was a most significant move. He constructed high walls and towers to fortify the area, and he stationed a Macedonian garrison there, in addition to Judeans who were loyal to Antiochus' policy. This "Akra" replaced the former city of Jerusalem, which had been partially depopulated and deprived of its enclosing wall.

About a year after Appolonius' activities, an order of Antiochus IV Epiphanes was promulgated prohibiting the Jewish faith.

The privileges that had been granted to the Jerusalem religious community from the beginning of the Persian period by the reigning emperors, and which had been repeatedly confirmed right up to the reigns of Antiochus III and Seleucus IV, and which guaranteed the community the right to live according to its own religious laws, were thereby abolished.

On 6 December 167 B.C.E., the Seleucid measures culminated in the dedication of the Jerusalem temple to Zeus Olympus and the construction of a pagan altar on top of the great altar of sacrifice in the Temple, which was dubbed "the abomination of desolation." [60] It was at this time, at the latest, that the daily sacrifice was discontinued, and on 15 December that the first offerings in honor of the king were presented. Antiochus now decreed that the pig should be sacrificed and circumcision banned.

---

[60] *Dan.* 11: 31; *Dan.* 12: 11

Jews consider the implementation of these royal orders and prohibitions "persecution."

The Antiochus IV Epiphanes was seen by the Judeans who resisted him to have attacked the foundation of Juda-ism, its major symbols of national identity, the High Priesthood and the cult.

Nevertheless, these actions did not represent a deliberate persecution of the Jews by the Seleucid government; rather, they were a form of retribution against disobedient subjects who had disobeyed the monarch and his appointed High Priest. The persecution was implemented as a consequence for the defiance of the royal edict by an obstinate people.

Due to Apollonius's actions and Antiochus Epiphanes' edicts, numerous individuals willingly faced death for their faith. Most, however, fled Jerusalem into the countryside, and a few took refuge in the desert and caves to avoid profaning their religion.[61]

Alongside the conflict between Israel and the Seleucid Empire, a further discord arose between the "pious" and the "apostates" within Yehud.

---

[61] *1 Macc.* 1: 38. *2 Macc.* 5: 27 relates the flight of Judah the Maccabee and his people from the city immediately after the actions of Apollonius and before those of Antiochus

The Hasmoneans

Mattathias, a priest of the tribe of Joarib, accompanied by his five sons, Yohanan, Simon, Judah, Eleazar, and Jonathan, was one of those who left Jerusalem to live in the small town of Modi'in on the road between Jerusalem and Jaffa, probably the family's ancestral home. The family called themselves 'Hasmonaeans' after Hasmon, their most recent ancestor.

To ensure that no one could avoid participating in the festivals of the new cult, temporary altars were now required to be placed in front of every house. The king's roving envoys arrived in Modi'in to ensure that all Jews followed the new faith's jurisdiction.

Mattathias not only refused to obey the order to offer sacrifice, saying

> *Even if all the nations that live under the rule of the king obey him and have chosen to do his commandments, departing each one from the religion of his fathers, I and my sons and my brothers will live by the covenant of our fathers.*[62]

He killed a Jew, who was willing to offer a sacrifice, as well as the royal official. He then destroyed the altar.

With this act, Mattathias raised the flag of revolt. It was now impossible for the Hasmonean family to stay in

---

[62] *1 Macc.* 2: 19 f.

Modi'in. He called on his fellow citizens to follow him and escape with him to the mountains in the inaccessible wilderness of Yehud. There, through 166 B.C.E., like-minded followers gathered around him.

Then many who were seeking righteousness and justice went down to the wilderness to dwell there: they, their sons, their wives, and their cattle, because evils pressed heavily upon them. And it was reported to the king's officers and to the troops in Jerusalem, the city of David, that men who had rejected the king's command had gone down to the hiding places in the wilderness.

Many pursued them and overtook them; they encamped opposite them and prepared for battle against them on the Sabbath day. And they said to them, "Enough of this! Come out and do what the king commands, and you will live." But they said, "We will not come out, nor will we do what the king commands and so profane the Sabbath day." Then the enemy hastened to attack them.

But they did not answer them or hurl a stone at them or block up their hiding places, for they said, "Let us all die in our innocence; heaven and earth testify for us that you are killing us unjustly." So, they attacked them on the sabbath, and they died, with their wives and children and cattle, to the number of a thousand persons.

When Mattathias and his friends learned of it, they mourned for them deeply. And each said to his neighbor, "If we all do as our brethren have done

*and refuse to fight with the Gentiles for our lives
and our ordinances, they will quickly destroy us
from the earth." So, they made this decision that
day: "Let us fight against every man who comes to
attack us on the sabbath day; let us not all die as
our brethren died in their hiding places."*

*Then there united with them a company of Hasidim,
mighty warriors of Israel, everyone who offered
himself willingly for the law. And all who became
fugitives to escape their troubles joined them and
reinforced them.*[63]

The aged Mattathias died shortly after he had organized
these guerrillas, and leadership was assumed by his third
son, Judah, surnamed the Maccabee.[64]

The Jewish resistance led by Judah and his brothers took
some time to get started. Initially, Judah avoided direct
combat with the Syrians. The first actions targeted
"apostate" Jews.

For two years, Judah waged guerrilla war like his father,
making surprise raids on the apostates without attacking
any walled cities or the tyrant's stronghold in Jerusalem.

He would now appear at Beth Horon (about five hours
northwest of Jerusalem), Modi'in, Mizpah, or on the

---

[63] *1 Macc.* 2: 29- 43

[64] The meaning of the name "Maccabee" is uncertain. The term is derived from
the Hebrew word *makkeb*, "mallet." It has also been believed to be an acrostic
of the Hebrew words which in translation mean: "Who is like unto Thee among
the gods, O Lord" (*Ex.* 15: 11). It has also been suggested, that it was originally
Juda's surname: "the hammer."

Samaritan border. The small band of organized guerrillas would fall at night upon the villages where altars had been erected and tore them down; they punished severely those Judeans who aided Antiochus' forces; they circumcised those who, following the king's decree, had not been circumcised.

Initially, the handful of strikes of the Maccabees could only be regarded as the actions of another robber band on the highways. The reality, however, was that its leaders' considerable tactical skill and its soldiers' fighting ability combined to form a powerful army that could not be destroyed by isolated failures.

What began as a religious crusade to restore Jewish worship soon turned into a war for an independent Jewish state, in which the Maccabean faction was only a minority movement for some of the time.

The first attempt to crush the revolt came from Apollonius, [65] whom Judah succeeded in defeating.

Then, for the first time, Judah met an organized army headed by Seron—the governor of Syria—at Bet Horon on the road to Jaffa, twelve miles northwest of Jerusalem. This was a large mercenary army that didn't fight with the same zeal as the Maccabees' soldiers, who won an important victory. [66]

---

[65] Though Apollonius was a very common name in the Hellenistic period, perhaps the same Apollonius who, according to *2 Macc.* 5: 24, had carried out the conquest and pillaging of the city of Jerusalem in the year 169 B.C.E. on behalf of Antiochus. NOTH, MARTIN: *The History of Israel*, p. 368

[66] Seron's casualties numbered about 800, while the rest of his army fled to the coast.

While this was going on in Yehud, the Parthians, a major Iranian political and military power in northeast Iran, rebelled against Antiochus IV Epiphanes, disrupting the direct trade route to India, and effectively splitting the Greek world in two. While Antiochus hurried off to fight the Parthians, he sent a commander named Lysias to deal with the Maccabees. He also made him guardian of his son, who was to succeed Antiochus as emperor.

With full power to stamp out the Judean revolt, Lysias decided to settle the rebellion of the Jews once and for all.

He assembled his best three army commanders: Ptolemy, Dorymenes' son; Nicanor; and Gorgias. Their forces included approximately 40,000 infantrymen and 7,000 cavalry.

Lysias remained in Antioch to manage the state's affairs. The crushing of the revolt appeared so certain that merchants from other countries joined the army, bringing fetters to chain the slaves they expected to buy from the Syrians."[67]

Though the Maccabee army was clearly inferior to the Syrian army led by three outstanding generals, they confronted the Syrian forces encamped at Emmaus, about twenty-two miles west of Jerusalem on the road to Jaffa, in September 165 B.C.E.

Gorgias decided to launch a surprise attack. Following nightfall, 5,000 infantrymen and a thousand cavalrymen

---

[67] ZEITLIN, SOLOMON: *The Rise and Fall of the Judaean State: A Political, Social and Religious History of the Second Commonwealth,* Vol. I. p. 98

marched toward Judah's camp. However, the Maccabees had spies in the Syrian army and were aware of Gorgias' plans. Judah's forces also attacked the main body of the Syrian army at night, surprising and annihilating them.

When Gorgias entered the Judaean camp and saw no one, he assumed Judah had fled to the mountains and pursued him. After marching all night in search of Judah and his men, Gorgias' forces returned to their camp at daybreak to find it in flames, with Judah and his men ready for battle. The Syrian army fled instead of attacking.

Judah's victory was complete. The war spoils were particularly rich due to the wealth brought by the foreign merchants in anticipation of buying the Judeans as slaves. [68]

The most significant consequence of Judah's victory was that the road was now open to Jerusalem.

Upon their return to Jerusalem, which was now open to them, the victors sang songs of thanksgiving, indicating that many of the songs that are now part of the book of *Psalms* were compiled by the men of Judah Maccabee and their successors after their victories.

It was the fall of 165 B.C.E., and Judah's forces now controlled the road from Jaffa to Jerusalem. The royal garrison of the Akra was now cut off from direct communication with the sea and thus with the government.

---

[68] *1 Macc.* 4: 1-27

Lysias recognized the serious consequences of the revolt if it was not crushed right away, as it could spread throughout the Seleucid Empire. Instead of invading from the north, he did it from the south by way of Idumaea. The route took him along the coast and to the south, bypassing the hilly regions, and eventuated in an encampment at Bet Zur which lies about twenty miles south of Jerusalem, toward Hebron. This was a large Seleucid force, certainly larger than the force sent during the Battle of Emmaus the previous year.

Judah was forced to quit his hiding place in the hills and hurry southward. He could now mobilize a substantial army; however, it was still insufficient to match the Lysiasians' numbers, as Judah lacked both cavalry and elephants.

A hit-and-run raid-style attack was conducted by the Judean forces, during which the rebels charged a portion of the camp in a dramatic clash. Lysias, consequently, implemented an orderly retreat. Deputies were dispatched by the Maccabees to negotiate an agreement with Lysias.

About the same time, Menelaus, the High Priest and head of the Hellenizers party, also intervened in the negotiations and appeared as a mediator between the king and the Jews.

A Roman embassy probably en route to Antioch took the Jews' part and persuaded them to formulate their demands quickly so that they themselves might present them to the king. In short,
it appears that all parties were concerned to make peace between the government and the Maccabean insurgents.

Epiphanes was at the moment engaged in a serious war in the East, the imperial treasury was again empty, and the question of whether the Jews would eat in accordance with or in opposition to their dietary laws must now have seemed of little consequence to the government.

And so, Epiphanes resolved to call a halt to the persecutions.

In a proclamation to the Jewish nation, he declared that he had been informed by Menelaus that the Jews who had fled from their homes—that is, those loyal to the ancient faith, amongst whom were the Maccabees—desired to return to their legal abodes. Exemption from punishment was guaranteed to all who returned by March 29, 164 B.C.E., and in addition, the assurance was given that the Jews would be permitted "to use their own food and to observe their own laws as of yore."

It had taken about three years for both the prohibitions against obeying the Torah and the *polis* constitution, which had been forced upon the people, to be rescinded. The persecution was thus ended.

For over a year, [69] the Syrians left Judea alone. Full independence, however, had not been achieved, nor was internal strife over. In the second half of the year 164 B.C.E., Judah and his followers felt sufficiently confident to march on Jerusalem and retake the Temple area, meeting no resistance.

---

[69] autumn 165 to spring 163

While the temple was cleansed and rededicated, Judah appointed a guard to keep the Syrian holed up in the Akra. This was the place where the leaders of the Hellenistic movement in Jerusalem had established their operational headquarters and from where they had controlled Jerusalem.

The Temple was now in Maccabee hands, but nothing happened for months. Weeds were growing in the temple courts as if they were in a forest, suggesting that there has been no activity there for an extended period. [70]

The Haredim believed that the fulfillment of the apocalyptic prophecies in the Book of Daniel and elsewhere was imminent. The Seleucid Empire would come to an end, and the eternal kingdom would be ushered in with the resurrection. These prophecies mentioned no *human* acts of restoration. Their position was that it would be presumptuous for humans to restore the Temple when God was about to do it.

According to the Haredim, God would act at the beginning of the sabbatical year, coming in the Jewish month of Tishrei in the year 164 B.C.E.

Out of respect for this view, Judah waited. Tishrei came and went, and no miraculous intervention took place.

While meeting the Haredim's objections, at the beginning of the Jewish New Year, [71]Judah destroyed the idol installed in the Temple, known as the "Abomination of

---

[70] *1 Macc.* 4: 38

[71] Tishrei

Desolation." This destruction was presented as an act of zeal for God and not as a permanent substitution of human action for God's work. He appointed priests who remained loyal to ancestral traditions who took apart the burnt offering altar, which had been defiled by pagan sacrifices, and put aside its stones. In its place, a new altar was constructed, and necessary cultic equipment was prepared.

Due to the absence of the artifacts found in the original Tabernacle and the First Temple, the Hasmoneans emphasized the significance of the Golden Menorah in their worship.

Judah waited till the end of Sukkot. [72] When no developments occurred, there seemed to be no reason to prolong their wait. However, they chose to hold off until the 25th day of Kislev [73] for the formal rededication of the Temple.

This delay was significant, as it marked the anniversary when Antiochus IV Epiphanes had erected the "Abomination of Desolation" in the Sanctuary and dedicated the Temple to Zeus Olympus. That day had brought the utmost humiliation for the Judeans. Now, three years later, the same date would witness a jubilant celebration of their remarkable victory.

---

[72] The seven-day holiday where Jews dwell in temporary huts called *sukkah* (pl. *sukkot*) commemorating the years the Israelites spent in the dessert after leaving Egypt. It is celebrated by shaking the four species, praising God for the Exodus from Egypt and the harvest.

[73] December 164 B.C.E.

···

Yehud was still surrounded by enemies on all sides.
Whenever they had the chance, the neighboring peoples
had gladly helped the Syrians fight against the Jews. They
had not only helped them with soldiers and money, but
they had also started to attack the Jews in their own midst.

The pagans of Jaffa, for example, drowned two hundred
Jews who lived among them. Other cities committed
similar atrocities. Everywhere the Jews outside of Judean
territory lived in constant danger of destruction.
Consequently, as soon as the Temple had been cleansed,
Judah decided to send punitive expeditions against the
Hellenized neighbors to prevent them from sending more
assistance to the Syrians when the latter renewed the war
against him, as it was expected they would do.

Judah, then, called a *Kneset haGedolah*, a Great
Assembly,[74] that directed him and his brother Simon to go
to Galilee and Jonathan to go to Gilead to save their
brethren from annihilation.

"Judah certainly had no intention of annexing territory to
Judea. On the contrary, wherever necessary, he led the
Jewish inhabitants back to their homeland."[75]

After the Maccabean brothers concluded their expeditions
in the spring of 164 B.C.E., Judah began the siege of the

---

[74] *1 Mac.* 5: 16

[75] GRAYZEL, SOLOMON: *A History of the Jews: From the Babylonian Exile to the Present*, p. 71

'Akra' in Jerusalem, where Menelaus and the Syrian garrison were stationed.

Menelaus and many of his followers, however, managed to escape. They fled to Antioch, where they claimed they had endured hardships for the sake of the king and suffered due to their adherence to the decrees of King Antiochus Epiphanes. They warned that the citadel was at risk of being captured and the garrison annihilated by Judah Maccabee unless aid arrived soon. They further cautioned that the entire country could fall into the hands of the Maccabees, stating, 'Unless you stop them at once, they will do more than this, and you will not be able to check them.'" [76]

Antiochus IV Epiphanes had just died during a campaign against the Parthians, and he was succeeded by his eight-year-old son Antiochus V Eupator, who was entirely dependent on his guardian, the regent Lysias. In the summer of 163 B.C.E., Lysias embarked once again on a second expedition against the Maccabees.

The course of the march was once again from the south through Idumea to Beth-Zur, to which Lysias laid siege. Judah left off his own siege of the Akra to meet the Syrians but was defeated in a battle near Beth-Zechariah. He then took back refuge in the temple, where he was besieged by Lysias.

The siege, however, didn't last long. Philip, the general who had been given authority by Antiochus IV on his deathbed, attempted a coup in Antioch, forcing Lysias to

---

[76] *1 Macc.* 6: 18- 24.

abandon Yehud and return to the Seleucid's capital to save his rule. He discontinued the siege of the temple and came to terms with the defenders.

In the young king's name, he offered peace to the besieged on the basis of an assurance of freedom to worship in accordance with the traditional law. All the orders issued by Antiochus IV Epiphanes in the year 167 B.C., which had led to the outbreak of the military conflict, were now officially rescinded, and the Jerusalem religious community was thereby restored to its old position.

On his way back from Yehud, Lysias ordered Menelaus executed, likely because he realized that no peace with the Jews would be possible as long as Menelaus continued to hold the office of high priest. After the execution, Alcimus was appointed to take Menelaus's place as High Priest.

Though the right to freely conduct public worship and daily life in accordance with the traditional law had been officially recognized, and a new high priest was once again in office, there was still a Seleucid garrison in the 'Akra' in Jerusalem, and Seleucid officials and troops were still present in the land. Yehud was still under foreign rule.

Judah and his followers were aiming at complete political independence and the complete elimination of foreign rule. They had no confidence in the peace and considered it intolerable that, for all his legitimacy, the new high priest had been appointed by the king with the aid of political and military resources in the same way as his immediate predecessors had been appointed by a hostile king.

On the other hand, for many Jews, the issue was simply one of religious freedom. For those Jews, only concerned with the freedom to practice their worship unhindered and with the right to live strictly in accordance with the law, once Antiochus V Eupator rescinded the decrees of his father, Antiochus IV Epiphanes, and restored to the Jews the right to live "according to their own laws, the time had come to be satisfied with what had been achieved. Ss soon as their freedom of religious worship was assured, the Hasidim, who had been with the Maccabees from the beginning of the revolt, deserted Judah and his comrades.

• • •

On learning of the death of Antiochus IV, Epiphanes, his nephew Demetrius, who was held hostage in Rome, escaped. [77]

Debarking at Tripoli, north of Sidon, the people of Syria and the army rallied to him. The boy king and the regent Lysias were put to death.

In the summer of 162, the High Priest Alcimus brought a formal complaint to Demetrius I, charging Judah and his followers with being warmongers and revolutionaries who not only wanted to deprive him of his high priesthood, which was his ancestral glory, but were also opposed to the king and were harming the country economically.

Judah and his brothers were called traitors to the state, and so Demetrius I appointed Bacchides, one of his friends, to

---

[77] 162 B.C.E.

march to Yehud to drive Judah and his followers out and to reinstate Alcimus as the high priest.

Left with a small group of supporters after the defection of the Hasidim, Judah Maccabee could not risk an open battle with Bacchides. He therefore left Jerusalem and went into the country.

Bacchides, thinking that he had succeeded in restoring Syrian control, returned to Antioch, leaving a small military force behind to protect Alcimus and supervise the affairs of Yehud.

But Judah continued to harass Alcimus and his supporters, so the High Priest again turned to Antioch for help.

Ptolemy, son of Dorymenes, the military commander of Syria and Phoenicia, appointed Nicanor and Gorgias to lead a larger force against the Maccabees. The expedition led by Nicanor is said to have included 40,000 foot soldiers and 7,000 cavalry.

Judas won an initial engagement at Caphar Salama, about 6 miles northwest of Jerusalem. Nicanor summoned additional reinforcements, and a battle ensued on the 13th of Adar, [78] near Adasa, 4 miles north of Jerusalem. Nicanor was defeated and killed in the battle; Judas was able to pursue the defeated enemy all the way down into the coastal plain. Judah had finally reached the pinnacle of his career with a brilliant victory over Nicanor.

However, this was far from the end of the story.

---

[78] March of 161 B.C.E.,

74

Bacchides returned with a massive army in April 160 B.C.E. to finally put an end to the Maccabean rebellion.

Following the Hasidim's defection, many of Judah's supporters saw engaging Bacchides forces as futile and opted out.

Despite being left with only 800 men, Judah went into battle and died there. His death marked the end of the first phase of the Maccabean struggle.

Those who had followed Judah Maccabee or were suspected of being sympathetic to his goal of establishing Judaea as an independent state were apprehended and tortured to death. Judah's remaining brothers, Simon, Jonathan, and Johanan, accompanied by several hundred Maccabean soldiers, fled to the wilderness of Tekoa, which stretches from southeast Bethlehem to the Dead Sea, and chose Jonathan as their leader.

• • •

Bacchides established a number of strongholds and occupied them with garrisons to secure the Seleucid rule in the land.

The aristocracy who followed the High Priest Alcimus were now in control of their countrymen. All Jonathan and his followers could do now was to repeatedly disrupt the peace in the land.

The High Priest Alcimus died, and with no available candidate who had the proper priestly genealogy, the post remained vacant.

In the summer of 160, Bacchides returned to Antioch, presenting Jonathan and his brother Simon with opportunities to harass the men who ruled in Jerusalem, ambushing and punishing those whom they considered friendly to the Syrian government. Recognizing Jonathan's growing strength, the leaders in Jerusalem appealed to Demetrius to send an army to put an end to Jonathan and his followers. At the invitation of Jonathan's foes, Bacchides returned once again to Yehud with a large army. [79]

Lacking the necessary force to repel the Syrians, Jonathan and his brother Simon withdrew to Bet Basi in the wilderness of Yehud some three miles east of Tekoa.

Learning that the Hasmoneans had occupied and fortified the village, Bacchides besieged it. Then Jonathan withdrew in secret, leaving Simon in charge of some of his men to keep the fight in Bet Basi as a distraction while he conducted expeditions against neighboring peoples. Many of them allied willingly with him against Bacchides. Thus, Jonathan succeeded in gathering a sufficient number of warriors to attack Bacchides from the wilderness while Simon did the same from the fortress.

Bacchides had not expected Jonathan's stubborn resistance nor attacks on two fronts. To cover up his failed attempt to

---

[79] 158 B.C.E.

destroy the Maccabees and save face, he blamed the leaders in Jerusalem and executed many of them.

Jonathan, sensing Bacchides' differences with his Judaean allies, saw this as an opportunity to reach an agreement with him. He sent ambassadors to Bacchides with a proposal for peace. Eager to return to Antioch, Bacchides accepted the offer. At Jonathan's request, he handed over the prisoners and the booty he had taken and desisted from further hostilities. He also agreed for Jonathan to remain as the leader of his group but would not permit him to reside in Jerusalem. As a result of this agreement, the Seleucid garrison on the Akra that ruled Jerusalem remained intact.

Jonathan went to Michmash, 8 miles northeast of Jerusalem, in 157 B.C.E., from where he ruled as if he was one of the old 'judges of Israel.'

Bacchides' gesture reaffirmed standard Seleucid policy: support for respected Jewish leaders who could maintain regional stability. The general regarded Jonathan as having attained that status.

After Bacchides left Yehud for Antioch, the leaders in Jerusalem no longer enjoyed the undivided support of the Syrian government. Moreover, their position was greatly weakened by the lack of a High Priest.

The war had now come to an end; the High Priest, position was left vacant. But for the time being, Jonathan evidently did not wish to enter that area of potential conflict. In any event, the empty berth at the head of the religious establishment demonstrated the Hasmoneans' precarious reputation among their own people.

Four years after Jonathan had established himself in Michmash, the reigning Seleucid king, Demetrius I, son of Seleucus IV, was challenged to the throne by Alexander Balas, who claimed to be Antiochus IV's son.

When Alexander Balas landed in Acco in the summer of 152, Demetrius I recognized the danger, and in order to ensure having Jonathan's support, conferred upon him the formal title of 'ally.'" The Seleucid king gave him official permission to maintain an armed unit and handed over to Jonathan the hostages who had been held in the 'Akra' in Jerusalem.

The status of ally meant acknowledgment of the Maccabean's standing as an autonomous political entity, and the extrication of hostages from the Akra effectively invited Jonathan to reenter Jerusalem.

Armed with these concessions, Jonathan moved to Jerusalem, refortified the area of the Temple, and kept the anxious garrison and occupants of the 'Akra' in check. The only other garrison that the Seleucids still maintained was the one in the fortress of Beth-zur.

But, at the same time, the pretender Alexander Balas was also seeking Jonathan's favor. He wrote to Jonathan with the salutation of "brother," accorded him the title of "friend of the king," a designation of high distinction in the Seleucid system, and most tellingly, appointed him as High Priest of the Jews.

Balas added a concrete element to his gesture by sending purple garb and a gold crown, the tokens of secular power, for Jonathan's investiture. The garment represented a Seleucid court practice that signaled that now Jonathan took on the role of Hellenistic courtier and royal official.

Seven years after the high priest Alcimus, a Seleucid appointee, and the last of the Aaronids died, the Hasmonean family, priests of a minor non-Zadokite, non-Aaronid branch, filled the vacancy themselves in the person of Jonathan, the youngest son of Mattathias.

Accordingly, in 152 B.C.E. the Zadokite priesthood was displaced from high-priestly office by the Hasmoneans, who would occupy this office until the reign of Herod.

Obviously, a considerable segment of the Judaeans opposed this appointment. The resistance came from two groups. Those who were partly Hellenized and had been followers of Jason, Menelaus, and Alcimus; and the Hasidim, who followed the laws of the Torah literally.

When, with Jonathan, the Hasmoneans ceased their struggle against the Seleucids and accepted the Hellenistic kingdom as their governors, they signaled that they were more interested in high office than in national sovereignty.[80]

Judas had raised a revolt against Antiochus IV's perverse policy but not against the Seleucid kingdom. He had never claimed as objective the eradication of Hellenistic power in Yehud, let alone of Hellenism.[81]

---

[80] BIALE, DAVID: *Power & Powerlessness in Jewish History*, p. 20

[81] GRUEN, ERICH, S.: *Heritage and Hellenism: The Reinvention of Jewish Tradition*, p. 16

Demetrius I fell in battle, and Alexander Balas became king of Syria and Babylonia.

The new king also framed a marriage alliance with Ptolemy VI Philometor of Egypt by marrying his daughter Cleopatra Thea. The wedding was celebrated with grand festivities at Ptolemais (Akko) in 150 B.C.E. Jonathan arrived in splendor for the ceremony in Ptolemais, brought expensive gifts for the two kings and for their friends, and found favor in their eyes. Jonathan's status as representative of the Jewish nation had now been openly proclaimed by two Hellenistic monarchs, and he had collected a package of titles and honors to overawe opponents at home.

In the year 147 B.C.E., the son of Demetrius I, also known as Demetrius, rebelled against Balas' position as king. The Seleucid Empire experienced a two-year civil war, which ended with Demetrius II killing Alexander Balas.

The turmoil in Syria gave Jonathan the opportunity of making Yehud an independent state.

The symbol of Yehud's subjugation to Syria was the Akra where a Syrian army contingent was stationed. Jonathan assembled his army and attacked the citadel.

Some Judaeans, however, were opposed to the establishment of an independent state under the leadership of the Hasmoneans, who were not of the high priestly or Davidic families. A delegation of these Judaeans went to see King Demetrius II to inform him of Jonathan's designs. The author of *1 Maccabees* calls these Judeans *"men who hated their nation.*"[82] Previous authors had termed such people "lawless men and sinners."

When Demetrius II learned of Jonathan's attack, he went to Ptolemais and called on Jonathan to abandon the siege of the citadel. He further commanded him to come to Ptolemais for a conference. Jonathan refused to lift the siege; however, he went to Ptolemais, taking with him a number of elders and priests. He also carried along a sizable amount of gold with which he hoped to mollify Demetrius' anger. The strategy was successful.

Jonathan succeeded in appeasing the kings' wrath, and instead of being punished for his behavior, he returned to Jerusalem with new concessions from the king.

Demetrius II not only explicitly confirmed him in his offices but also confirmed the privileges of the Jerusalem religious community. He also handed over to him the three southern districts of the province of Samaria, whose inhabitants had remained loyal to the cultus of nearby Jerusalem and did not take part in the Samaritan cultus on Gerizim. In this way Yehud was enlarged by a wide strip of land northwards and northwestwards.

Though even if these concessions testified to both Jonathan's diplomatic abilities and Demetrius II's sense of insecurity on his throne, Demetrius II was not prepared to withdraw the Seleucid garrison from the Akra in Jerusalem and from Beth Zur.

---

[82] *1 Macc.* 11: 20

Diodotus Tryphon, who had been a military leader in the army of Alexander Balas, was in the meantime fighting to win the Seleucid throne for the son of Alexander Balas and rule the empire through him.

Tryphon offered to make Jonathan's brother Simon governor of the Mediterranean coast from Egypt to Tyre. This appointment would provide Jonathan with many opportunities to consummate his ambitions: to free Yehud, enlarge her territory, and, particularly, to add those cities that would give her an outlet to the Mediterranean. Jonathan, who had alienated himself from Demetrius II because of his refusal to give up the two garrisons still in Yehud, therefore joined Tryphon and became his ally.

With his brother Simon, they launched a series of successful campaigns that extended from the southern coastal plain as far as Galilee and the region of Damascus.

Jonathan also took steps to strengthen his position diplomatically. He sent an embassy to Rome to confirm and renew the treaty of friendship between them. And he also sent an embassy of friendship to the Spartans.

Furthermore, he built new strongholds in Yehud. He strengthened and raised the wall of Jerusalem and built a high wall between the Syrian-occupied Akra of Jerusalem and the rest of the city to make interference from the Akra impossible.

Tryphon could not allow Jonathan's increase of power to go unpunished.

Commanding a small army, Tryphon met Jonathan at the head of a 40,000-man army in Scythopolis. To remove any suspicion from Jonathan's mind, Tryphon bestowed many honors upon Jonathan and insisted that his strong army was superfluous since they were friends. He advised Jonathan to disperse his forces and send the men home, and he offered to accompany him to Ptolemais.

Although Ptolemais was outside the borders of Judaea, it had been given to Jonathan by Demetrius I. Tryphon promised to recognize Jonathan as the official owner of the city and also to present to him the entire coast from Ptolemais to Jaffa. The offer was irresistible.

Jonathan dismissed his army, retaining only a small troop, and accompanied Tryphon to Ptolemais. When Jonathan and his retinue entered the city, they were arrested; the soldiers were slain, and he was taken prisoner.

Tryphon left Ptolemais with an army to invade Judaea, carrying Jonathan with him as a hostage. Simon came to meet him encamping in Adida, about four miles northeast of Lydda.

Tryphon sent word to Simon that he bore no malice either toward him or his brother Jonathan. He explained that he held Jonathan as a hostage only because Jonathan had not made payment to the royal treasury for the office he was occupying. He said that if Simon would send him 100 talents of silver and two of Jonathan's sons as hostages, he would free his brother.

In order not to be accused of having brought about Jonathan's death, Simon forwarded the money and sent along his two nephews, the sons of Jonathan. Though the demands were met, Jonathan was not freed.

Seeing the strong position of Simon's army in Adida, Tryphon decided not to attack and marched on Jerusalem. Due to an unusually heavy snowfall, the roads became hazardous, especially for the cavalry. Tryphon gave up his march against the city and turned to the south, proceeding to the extreme end of the Dead Sea and thence east of the Jordan to Gilead. There he had Jonathan executed, and he returned to Syria.

Eighteen years after his brother Judah had fallen in battle, Jonathan was treacherously killed.

When Judah Maccabee died, there was hardly an army to speak of. There were guerilla fighters and fanatics who were ready to sacrifice their lives for their beliefs; Jonathan succeeded in forming a regular army. He was more than a great organizer; he was a fine statesman. He knew how to use the weakness of the Seleucid Empire to Yehud's advantage. He took sides in the Syrian civil wars in such a way as to improve Yehud's position and his own as its leader. [83]

• • •

After the death of Jonathan, of the five sons of Mattathias, only Simon was left. He became the leader of the Hasmonean movement.

---

[83] ZEITLIN, SOLOMON: *The Rise and Fall of the Judaean State: A Political, Social and Religious History of the Second Commonwealth,* Vol. I, p. 142

Simon buried his brother Jonathan beside his parents and his four brothers in the city of Modi'in. Later he built them a common sepulcher and set up seven pyramids in memory of his parents and four brothers.

In the first year of his reign, Simon conducted negotiations with Demetrius II Nicator, king of Syria, who officially recognized Judea's freedom, calling Simon 'High Priest and Friend of Kings' and granting exemption from taxes and the right to maintain fortresses.

The Great Assembly, which convened in Jerusalem two years later, recognized the Hasmoneans as a dynasty of ethnarchs, High Priests, and military commanders in Yehud.

1 Maccabees thus declared that 'the yoke of the Gentiles was removed from Israel.' [84]

The high priesthood that had been hereditary and confined to the family of Zadok for many centuries was now granted to Simon until a "true prophet should appear in Israel." [85]

Simon, however, was not of the family of Zadok, and thus the high priesthood and the leadership of the Jews were given by the Great Synagogue to someone outside of the hereditary line. The ancient Hellenizing aristocracy, which had been in control of land and the Temple till 168 B.C.E., now gave way to the Hasmonean house.

---

[84] 1 *Macc.* 13: 41- 42

[85] *1 Macc.* 14: 41-47

A whole new era began, marked by a dating scheme that commenced with the first year of Simon. Documents and contracts now began: "In the year one of Simon, great high priest, military commissioner, and leader of the Jews."

With his popular backing and a temporary calm, Simon was in a position to continue his brother's efforts to affect the independence of the state by building fortresses and preparing stores of food in case of protracted war.

He increased his power by capturing the strategically important town of Gezer, which lay on the road between Jaffa and Jerusalem, expelling the pagan residents, and placing a Jewish garrison in the city under the command of his son Yohanan.

At the same time, he showed his statesmanship with his clever diplomacy to safeguard Yehud's sovereignty, renewing relations with Sparta, and concluding a political alliance with the Romans.

On the 23rd day of Iyar, in the spring of 142, Simon's men entered the Akra, the last stronghold of the Hellenizers and their Syrian supporters, singing hymns to God and bearing palm branches as a sign of victory.

Nevertheless, the Seleucids had not given up their claims.

Demetrius II Nicator undertook an expedition against the Parthians in the east, in which he was taken prisoner by the Parthians. Thereupon, in 138 B.C.E., his brother, Antiochus VII Sidetes, set himself on the throne in Antioch and defeated the usurper Diodotus Tryphon at Dora.

The new Syrian king opposed Yehud's independent status and was particularly infuriated by Simon's attempt to enlarge the country's borders. He demanded of him the restoration to Syria of the towns of Jaffa and Gezer, also of the Akra fortress, or the payment of a sum of money in exchange for them.

Simon responded saying, "We have not taken foreign soil, but the inheritance of our fathers, which fell into the hands of our foes unjustly, and now the land has returned to its first owners."
In other words, in rejecting Sidetes' demands, Simon made it clear that he believed the Hasmoneans should rule over all of Yehud.

When Simon offered only one hundred talents for Jaffa and Gazara, Antiochus VII Sidetes response was to appoint General Cendebeus as commander of the coastal district, with orders to invade Yehud. Simon, who was too old to lead battles, sent his sons Judah and Yohanan to fight Sidetes. They defeated him decisively and burned Ashdod.

Simon had a son-in-law named Ptolemy, who was governor of the plains of Jericho. Presumably an assimilated Jew since he called himself by the traditional name of the Egyptian kings.

In the month of Shebat, 136 B.C.E., when Simon was making the rounds of the country, he visited Jericho with his wife and two sons, Judah and Mattathias; Yohanan was not with them, having remained in Gazara where he was in command. Ptolemy gave his guests a hospitable reception and escorted them to the fortress of Dok, which he had built. He entertained them and, during a banquet, had Simon and his two sons slain.

Judah had died without sons. Hence the great role of Mattathias and Simon as fathers of the Hasmonean dynasty. Simon had served as a father to the brothers, who have sought his counsel. He had demonstrated remarkable statesmanship from the beginning of the revolt until the establishment of the free state of Yehud, and now the mantle fell upon his remaining son, Yohanan Hyrcanus.

Following this perfidious betrayal, Ptolemy sent a letter to Antiochus asking for an army to be sent to him so he could annex Syria.

Ptolemy had taken his mother-in-law hostage after assassinating his father-in-law. When Yonathan attacked Dok, Ptolemy took her out upon the walls of Dok and threatened to throw her down to her death unless Yohanan Hyrcanus abandoned the siege. Yohanan would not allow his mother to die and lifted the siege. He then rushed away to Jerusalem to forestall Ptolemy's attempt to seize the capital and dominate the country.

In order to avenge the defeat of Cendebeus, Antiochus VII Sidetes invaded Yehud in 133 B.C.E., devastating the country before laying siege to Jerusalem.

This was a sabbatical year, and a severe food and water shortage began to manifest itself. Yohanan was eventually forced to give up and sue for peace.

The Jews agreed to all terms except the imposition of a garrison. They could not stand the thought of another Akra.

However, they offered substantial compensation in the form of cash and hostages, as well as the surrender of all weapons, taxes for Joppa and all other cities outside of Yehud, and the dismantling of the city walls' "crowns."

In comparison to the actions of Antiochus IV Epiphanes, Antiochus VII imposed relatively mild conditions. Despite having the Judaean state at his command and the ability to seize all of their possessions, including their independence, he was content with these modest demands.

Antiochus VII Sidetes had been planning strategies to retake the Upper Lands from the Parthians and was eager to launch the campaign in the north; however, the siege of Jerusalem had lasted longer than expected, forcing him to reach an agreement with Yohanan Hyrcanus. However, an additional reason for Antiochus VII's leniency may have been the Roman support for Yohanan Hyrcanus. The Romans, as part of their agreement with Simon, had committed themselves to defend the Judeans in the event of an attack, and the Syrian king did not wish to arouse the Romans' displeasure, particularly now.

Although it remained independent after the peace treaty was signed, Yehud became, in practice, a Syrian satellite.

In 133 BCE, Sidetes, accompanied by an army from Judea, set out to retake the former Seleucid lands in the Iranian East.

The Parthian campaign was disastrous. Antiochus VII Sidetes was defeated, and almost his entire army of 300,000 was wiped out; he was killed in the Battle of Ecbatana in 129 B.C.E. The Parthians subsequently recaptured all of the eastern territories. The Seleucid Dynasty fragmented and ultimately vanished with the Roman conquest of all of Asia Minor.

Yehud was free again.

The Seleucid state was so substantially weakened by the military failure of the Parthian campaign and the death of Antiochus VII that the Syrian display of strength in Judaea had merely been a brief interlude.

Freed from Seleucid domination, Hyrcanus set out to enlarge his kingdom at the expense of the crumbling Seleucid Empire.

Marching into the southern land east of the Jordan, he captured the city of Medeba, laying his hands on the country of *el-Belka,* which under David had been part of the kingdom of Israel. He did this by using mercenaries. King David had used mercenaries in the past because it was part of the strategy with which he was familiar; with Yonathan Hyrcanus, it was a sign of his lack of popular support. [86]

Deuteronomic Law, which was now the land's basic constitution, forbade conscription. Following the practice in the Hellenistic world, where the ruler stood above the state he ruled and whose power was independent from the population, Yonathan imported mercenaries from abroad for his army.

---

[86] NOTH, MARTIN: *The History of Israel*, p. 386

90

According to Josephus, the Hasmonaean king obtained money to pay for his army by opening King David's tomb and taking from it 300 talents of silver.

A long Jewish tradition marks the twenty-first day of the month of Kislev, the day when the Samaritan temple was destroyed, as a propitious day in the Hebrew calendar, on which it is forbidden to fast or mourn the dead. The national memory, too, honors the figure of Yonathan Hyrcanus, the Jewish Titus, destroyer of the Samaritan temple. Today in Israel, many streets proudly bear the name of his victorious Hasmonean priest." [87]

After taking Samaria, he overran the province of Idumaea (Edom'), which adjoined Judaea in the south and a territory that had belonged to Yehud until 598 B.C.E.

After subduing all the Idumaeans, Yonathan permitted them to remain in their country so long as they had themselves circumcised and were willing to observe all the laws of the Jews. And so, out of attachment to the land of their fathers, they submitted to circumcision and to making their manner of life conform in all other respects to that of the Jews. [88]

In this way, the frequent danger of sudden raids that had threatened Judea from the south became a thing of the past.

The Hasmonean victory, with its restoration of almost the whole Davidic kingdom, seemed at first a final and complete solution to the problems of the Jewish nation. The enlargement of the nation's territory and, in particular,

---

[87] SAND, SHLOMO: *The Invention of the Jewish People*, p. 160
[88] JOSEPHUS, FLAVIUS: *The Antiquities of the Jews*, 13. 9. 1 §§257- 58

access to the sea (both of which Judaea had lacked in the Persian and Hellenistic periods) ensured the nation's future also in the material sense. [89]

The Hasmonean rulers understood clearly that a state could not survive if it followed a way of life that was planned for a Persian province four centuries earlier. As they progressively consolidated their rule, the Hasmoneans had moved further and further from the original goals of the Maccabean movement.

By this time, Yonathan Hyrcanus had become thoroughly Hellenized and was disliked by the people of Yehud.

For the great mass of the people, the political and military necessities of the state were not as clear to them as to the kings, who had gained practical experience in the difficulties of administration and warfare. [90]

Developments were almost of necessity headed in the direction of a conflict between the ruling family and the religious parties.

Yonathan invited Pharisee sages, (the 'separate ones')—descendants in the direct line of the Hasidim from the early days of the revolt—to a banquet, during which he requested they outline to him all his errors and transgressions. All praised him highly, but one of the Pharisees, named Eleazar, rose and said, "If you desire to pursue the path of righteousness, you should give up the

[89] AVI-YONAH, M.: *The Jews under Roman and Byzantine Rule: A Political History of Palestine from the Bar Kokhba War to the Arab Conquest*, p. 5
[90] *ibid.*

High Priesthood and content yourself with ruling the nation only."

The high priesthood had lost its moral authority in the eyes of the people due to the assimilationist policy of Jason and Menelaus, who were members of the old Zadokite family. Subsequently, the priests found the Hasmonean kings to be intolerable. In the two centuries that preceded the common era, religious authority was gradually and definitively transferred to the emerging new class of scribes and sages, the Pharisees.

The Pharisees resisted the Hasmonean appropriation of the monarchy and High Priesthood due to their lack of the Davidic and Aaronic qualifications mandated by tradition; they also opposed them on political and socioeconomic grounds, citing their indulgence in opulence and the harshness of their treatment of adversaries.

Josephus states that Yohanan was in conflict with the Pharisees and oppressed them. And, after he was told by Eleazar the Pharisee that he should surrender the High Priesthood, Hyrcanus allied himself with the Sadducees. Josephus adds that, immediately after the split, Hyrcanus abolished all the laws that the Pharisees gave to the people.

Despite the fact that the Pharisees were in revolt against him, he served as ruler and High Priest for thirty-one years. He died in the summer of 105 B.C.E.

At his death, Hyrcanus left behind a state that, in addition to the Jewish heartland, included the most important cities of the coastal plain in the west, Samaria in the north, parts of Transjordan in the east, and Idumaea in the south.

The death of Yonathan Hyrcanus marks a significant change in Judaean history. With his successors, what had been a commonwealth became a monarchy.

The Hasmonean dynasty that had begun as the leadership of a people's rebellion now evolved into a ruling house that was autocratic, self-seeking, and widely despised; in short, a typical petty royalty of the Middle East—with its intrigues, treachery, and civil conflicts. [91]

$$\bullet \; \bullet \; \bullet$$

Yonathan Hyrcanus had formally left the rule of the country to his wife, but Aristobolus, his eldest son, seized the government, imprisoned his mother, and left her to die of starvation. He also put his brothers in prison, with the exception of Antigonus, who had been his comrade-in-arms and to whom he was devoted.

Aristobolus and his brother Antigonus had conquered Samaria together while their father was still alive. They had laid siege to the city, and when the inhabitants requested aid from the Seleucid Empire, they defeated a relief army led by Antiochus IX Cyzicenus. Antiochus successfully escaped to Scythopolis, [92] but the brothers captured Samaria towards the end of Yonathan Hyrcanus' reign, razing the city and enslaving its inhabitants. Their forces subsequently captured Scythopolis and the entire region south of Mount Carmel.

---

[91] ZEITLIN, SOLOMON: *The Rise and Fall of The Judaean State: A Political, Social and Religious History of the Second Commonwealth,* Vol. I. p. 317

[92] Today's Beth Shean, located 17 miles (27 km) south of the Sea of Galilee

Now, in a bid to Judaize the Galilee, Aristobolus fought the local population of Ituraeans whose kingdom was in Chalcis in Lebanon.

In ancient times, when the Greeks and Romans conquered a city, they either slaughtered all the people or sold them into slavery. Aristobulus, acting in a somewhat more humane manner, gave them the choice either to remain in the land on condition that they submit to circumcision and live in accordance with the laws of the Judaeans or else to be expelled. Many of them accepted the terms, and thus this region became a part of Yehud.

There is no question that significant differences in background, outlook, and observance were long to distinguish the Galilean from their southern compatriot. However, masses of these original inhabitants of the Galilee assimilated into the expanding Judean population, and many became devout Jews.

The territory annexed by Aristobulus stretched from Bet She'an (Scythopolis) in the south to beyond Giscala in the north—that is, most of today's Galilee minus the coast.

After defeating the Ituraeans and consolidating his power, Aristobolus converted the government from a commonwealth to a monarchy. In fact, he was the first Hasmonean to claim the title of king.

Josephus wrote that he was the first Jew in "four hundred and eighty-three years and three months to have established a monarchy since the return from the Babylonian captivity. This action widened the schism between him and the

Pharisees, who were fiercely anti-monarchy and especially despised a Hasmonean king.

In this shift toward a more Hellenistic form of government, Aristobulus completed a long-term development that had begun under his father, Hyrcanus.

"It was not by chance that Aristobulus, like his brothers, had a Greek name in addition to his Hebrew name (Jehudah) and that Josephus explicitly called him a 'Philhellen' (friend of the Greek.[93]

Salome, his wife, later known as Alexandra, was aware of the fate that had befallen her mother-in-law and brothers-in-law when Aristobolus first became ruler. Fearing for her own safety should her brother-in-law Antigonus become king, she engineered a conspiracy to murder him.

Antigonus had returned to Jerusalem from the battlefield to celebrate the festival of Sukkot at the Temple. Hearing that his brother, who suffered from chronic abdominal pains, was lying ill in the fortress of Baris went to visit him.

In his gloomy state, Aristobulus fell prey to the factious influence of his wife, Queen Salome Alexandra. The king was informed by "evil men" that his brother was sending soldiers to murder him.

Aristobulus, then, sent messengers to Antigonus summoning him to come unarmed. He gave orders to his guards that if Antigonus should pass Caesarea unarmed, they should allow him to proceed, but if Antigonus should come armed, they would kill him.

---

[93] *Ant.* XIII, 318.

The queen changed the king's message to Antigonus, ordering the messenger to say that the king wished him to come armed. Antigonus complied with this message. On passing Straton's Tower, he was murdered by the guards.

When Aristobulus learned of the assassination of his brother, he was so overcome with remorse that he suffered a severe hemorrhage, and he died.

Aristobulus I, Yonathan Hyrcanus' son, ruled for only one year. [94]

● ● ●

Aristobulus' wife, Salome Alexandra, now released the three imprisoned brothers of the dead king from prison and appointed one of them as king. His native name was Jonathan, but he was called by his pet name, Jannai, and only used his native name as a surname to a Greek name, so he became known as Alexander Jannaeus.

His father, Yonathan Hyrcanus, hated him from infancy and banished him to Galilee in early childhood. [95] A deep-seated insecurity and hatred persisted within him, and he was suspicious of the loyalty of every Judaean, particularly of the intellectuals. [96]

---

[94] (104- 103).

[95] *Ant* 13. 12, 1 (321)

[96] ZEITLIN, SOLOMON: *The Rise and Fall of the Judaean State. A Political, Social and Religious History of the Second Commonwealth,* Vol I, p. 321

On becoming king, he put the elder of his remaining brothers to death. This would indicate that Alexander Jannaeus was not entitled to succeed his father.

Since Aristobulus died childless, Jewish law required his widow to contract a levirate marriage with his brother, so Jannaeus married Salome Alexandra, his sister-in-law. He was twenty-two years old, while she was thirty-seven. "Salome thus achieved what she had planned. She not only saved her own life and continued as queen but also gained the power to choose one of the brothers as successor to her husband.

The political map of Asia Minor was undergoing significant revision in this period. Two powers emerged in the East: Armenia, whose armies overflowed Syria, and Pontus, which for a while became a strong power. From the south, the Nabateans also emerged as an important people. At the same time, Rome's influence in Africa and Asia was growing.

Jannaeus knew that the Seleucid monarchies in Syria were crumbling and that a great opportunity had come for Yehud to engage in conquest so as to become a strong state in Asia Minor.

At this time Judaea possessed only one port, Jaffa. Ptolemais and Straton's Tower (Caesarea), important ports on the Mediterranean Sea, were outside of Yehud.

After consolidating his rule, Jannaeus Alexander attacked Ptolemais [97]. This city was a logical choice for the

---

[97] biblical Acco

beginning of Judaea's conquests, not only because it was an important port but also because of its large population and its sandy beach, which provided material for glass manufacturers. Equally important, however, Ptolemais had been formally ceded to the Temple by Demetrius I, which gave Alexander Jannaeus grounds for claiming it.

The citizens of Ptolemais decided to seek help from Egypt. They did not call on Cleopatra III, who reigned in Egypt, however, but on her son Ptolemy, who ruled in Cyprus.

When Ptolemy arrived with an army, Alexander Jannaeus retired to Yehud. He proposed a friendly alliance with Ptolemy, but having no faith in the professed friendship and unsure of the benefits of the alliance, he secretly requested Cleopatra III's assistance against her son. When Ptolemy discovered that Alexander Jannaeus had asked his mother for assistance, he resolved to launch war against Yehud.

Ptolemy made a sudden attack on the city of Asochis, took it by storm, and captured 10,000 persons. He then attacked the city of Sepphoris. Alexander Jannaeus, learning of Ptolemy's ravaging of Galilee, moved with a strong army to counter him. The two met near a place called Asophon, which lies on the east bank of the Jordan. They were arrayed on opposite sides of the river.

When Ptolemy's men began to cross. Alexander Jannaeus did not place obstacles to this maneuver, thinking it would be easier to destroy them if the river were behind them. This strategy, however, turned out to be disastrous. At first, Alexander Jannaeus's army had the advantage, but later, by a clever maneuver of Ptolemy's generals, the Hasmonean king's army was forced to run.

Ptolemy's army followed in pursuit and smote the Judaeans "until their swords became blunted with slaughter and their hands were utterly weary." Alexander Jannaeus was no longer a force to be reckoned with.

Ptolemy captured many cities. He ordered the soldiers to cut the throats of the women and infants, to chop their bodies into pieces and fling them into boiling cauldrons, and to taste the contents. This was done so that those who succeeded in escaping would tell their fellows that the enemy were cannibals. Thus, the Judeans would be too terrified to oppose him.

After Ptolemy conquered Ptolemais and then Gaza, his mother, Cleopatra, could not sit back and watch her son rise to power. She was concerned that he would align himself with Antiochus IX Cyzicenus. She marched against him with an army led by two Judeans, Chelkias and Ananias, sons of Onias III, the high priest who built the Heliopolis' temple.

When Cleopatra's army was busy besieging Ptolemais, Ptolemy decided it was the right time to march against Egypt because his mother and her army were out of the country. However, Cleopatra dispatched a portion of her army, led by Chelkias, to oppose him, forcing him to flee. Chelkias died during this battle.

Cleopatra captured Ptolemais and became mistress of all Coele-Syria as a result of her victory. Some of her counselors advised her to annex Yehud, but Ananias, her commander-in-chief, persuaded her not to. He contended that doing so would not only be an injustice to the people of Yehud but would also alienate the Judaeans of Egypt. They had been her staunch allies in her fight against her son. Cleopatra followed his advice and returned to Egypt.

The young state of Yehud had been at the point of destruction. All the sacrifices and struggles of the Hasmoneans to establish it as an independent state would have come to naught had Cleopatra seen fit to act. But Yehud was saved through the influence of Judaeans in the Egyptian court who helped dissuade Cleopatra from annexing it. The state had been saved by its diaspora coreligionists." [98]

When Ptolemy was out of Yehud, Alexander Jannaeus felt once again free enough to continue his policy of conquest. He crossed the Jordan, and after a ten-month siege, he took Gadara, situated east of the junction of the Yarmuk and Jordan rivers.

He then captured the city of Amathus. This victory was costly, for 10,000 of his army were killed. He nonetheless marched to the west and besieged Raphia, which is about twenty miles southwest of Gaza on the border of Egypt, and captured it. Then, he moved against and captured the city of Anthedon, which lies north of Gaza.

Gaza was a major point on the coastal caravan route, being situated about two and a half miles from the Mediterranean. After having conquered the territory to the

---

[98] ZEITLIN, SOLOMON: *The Rise and Fall of the Judaean State. A Political, Social and Religious History of the Second Commonwealth*, Vol I, p. 323- 325

south and to the north of it, Alexander Jannaeus decided to take Gaza.

The siege lasted a year, but the end came swiftly. His army at first conducted itself with restraint. However, its urge to take revenge was intense, due to the penuries they endured during the long siege. Alexander Jannaeus then released his forces, and a bloody massacre followed, though the people of Gaza defended themselves heroically. The councilmen of the city, 500 in number, took refuge in the temple of Apollo. But the men of Alexander Jannaeus fell upon them there, and they were killed as their temple was burned over them.

Within Yehud, Sadducees and Pharisees, who had now evolved into political parties, were fighting each other on political grounds.

The Sadducees advocated for expansion, the incorporation of other Hellenistic communities, and the coercion of their people into accepting the Judaean religion.

On the other hand, Alexander Jannaeus faced strong Pharisaic opposition because they believed he had turned Yehud into a secular kingdom.

They regarded him as a Hellenistic ruler who was only Jewish by birth. They were opposed to expansion and the integration of foreign people, fearing that assimilating Hellenistic communities would dilute the Judaean religion. The Pharisees, to be sure, supported proselytism, but only through propaganda and education, not by force.

Furthermore, they feared that the conquest of new territories inhabited by Syrians and Greeks would demoralize the Jews. Wars also required the hiring of mercenaries, which resulted in taxing the people heavily.

The conflict between the Pharisees and Alexander Jannaeus resulted in open rebellion on their part, as well as atrocities and vengeful acts on the part of the king. He saw the Pharisees as not only personal enemies but also traitors to the cause of Yehud's expansion and development as a strong state capable of withstanding attack. These opposing attitudes resulted in a clash that eventually sowed the seeds of Yehud's civil wars, leading ultimately to the destruction of the Second Jewish Commonwealth.

One year during Sukkot, his Jewish opponents began to revile him and to throw *etrogim* [99] at him. The result was that six thousand Jews were executed. [100]

Alexander Jannaeus had always distrusted the people. Now that there was an open breakdown between him and them, he would not allow the people to be near him in the Temple. He had a barrier erected around the altar and, in addition, a barrier around the part of the Temple where only priests were permitted to enter; thus, he was doubly isolated from the people while he was in Yehud's sacred place.

As the civil war became more intense, the opposition appealed to Demetrius III (Eukairos) for aid.

---

[99] Citrons, the citrus fruit that features in the festival
[100] *War* 1.89; *Antiq.* 13. 372- 373

The Pharisees' invitation to a Syrian king—a great-grandnephew of Antiochus Epiphanes—to invade their country crossed all boundaries.

Demetrius III was engaged in conflict with his brother Philip over the Syrian crown, while Antiochus X, the progeny of Antiochus Cyzicenus, also vied for the same kingdom. With Demetrius III still engaged in the struggle for control of Syria, the Pharisees believed he would be unable to establish a stronghold in Judaea.

The Judeans who had invited Demetrius III to aid them against Alexander Jannaeus were those who still opposed a commonwealth, who believed in a theocratic form of community, and who were willing to live under foreign political domination, providing they had religious freedom as their ancestors had had for centuries under the Persians and later under the Ptolemies.

Demetrius III and his army responded to the invitation. Joined by many Judeans, they encamped near the city of Shechem. Alexander Jannaeus and his army, consisting of mercenaries and about 20,000 Judaeans, came out to meet them. To avert an attack from the east by the Nabataeans, the Hasmonean monarch yielded large territories, which he had previously conquered in Moab and Galaaditis, as a bribe to their king. This was an overwhelming humiliation to the Hasmonean since these territories were of great importance as a bulwark for the defense of Yehud.

The battle was decisive. Demetrius III was victorious. Jannaeus lost his army and fled for safety to the mountains.

Demetrius III, pressed by the advance of his brother Philip in Syria, had to withdraw. Many Judaeans continued to fight Alexander Jannaeus even after Demetrius III had left for Syria. In these battles many of them were slain. Their leaders took refuge in the city of Bethoma, ten miles northeast of Samaria, where they were besieged by Alexander Jannaeus, captured, and brought back to Jerusalem.

Jannaeus, who by nature was full of hatred, had a desire to take revenge upon his victims that was doubly intense. He derived extraordinary personal satisfaction from observing the torture of his enemies. When his victims, numbering 800, were brought to Yehud, he ordered their crucifixion, and while the victims were still alive, he had their wives and children slain before their eyes. He watched this barbarous procedure while eating and drinking with his concubines.

The civil war, during which 50,000 Judeans were killed, lasted six years. [94] After his victory over the Pharisees, 8,000 of them fled the country for safety outside the borders of Judaea. Alexander Jannaeus was now without opposition. He had the loyalty of the army, consisting mostly of mercenaries, the devotion of the top echelon of the military caste, as well as the Sadducees.

In the last three years of his life, Alexander Jannaeus was ill with quartan fever. He also became addicted to heavy drinking, probably to soothe his physical and mental sufferings. He died while besieging Ragaba across the Jordan. His wife, Salome, was with him at his camp.

Alexander Jannaeus reigned twenty-seven years and died at the age of forty-nine, in the year 78 B.C.E.

According to Josephus, towards the end of his reign, the dominions of the "Judaeans" embraced more or less the territories of the old kingdoms of Judah and Israel over which David and Solomon had ruled, and also the former land of the Philistines and the coast road to Egypt.[101]

He left two sons—Hyrcanus II [102] and Aristobulus II—but on his deathbed he entrusted the government, not to them, but to his wife, Salome Alexandra.

To keep the throne safe for herself and her children, the king had advised her to conceal his death until the fortress at Ragaba was captured. Once that was accomplished, she should engage the Pharisees and grant them specific powers so as to be positively disposed toward her. [103]

The queen had put Jannaeus in power and survived him. She seems to have anointed herself, given that her elder son, Hyrcanus II, should have been the one to succeed his father.

Her ascension to the throne would have been inconceivable in a society that held women in contempt. She would be one of only three women, [104] to rule over Israel,

---

[101] *Ant. Iud.* XIII, 15, 4, §§ 395-397

[102] Yonathan Hyrcanus II

[103] *Ant.* 13.15.5 (400-403). Jannaeus' testament to his wife Salome is given in the Talmud in a different but complementary version (*Sota* 22).

[104] the other two being Deborah, the fourth Judge of pre-monarchic Israel, and Athaliah daughter of King Ahab and Queen Jezebel of Israel (841-835 B.C.E.)

establishing her reign as a significant chapter in the annals of Jewish leadership.

Salome fulfilled the request of her late husband and, during her discussions with the Pharisee leaders, provided them with the assurances they required to agree to treat Alexander's remains with the respect he was entitled to as a king.

All of the Pharisees' laws were reinstated, cementing their position as the power elite in Yehud.

Tradition has it that Salome Alexander was the sister of Simon ben Shetah [105], leader of the Pharisees and head of the Sanhedrin.

> "These Pharisees artfully insinuated themselves into her favor little by little and became themselves the real administrators of the public affairs: they banished and reduced whom they pleased; they bound and loosed [men] at their pleasure; [106]

The most significant aspect of her reign was, in fact, her total reversal of domestic policy, as testified by the agreement she carried with the Pharisees. For this reason, she is called in Jewish tradition "Shlomtzion," [107] her Hebrew name, rather than by her Greek name Salome Alexander.

---

[105] *Ber* 48

[106] JOSEPHUS, FLAVIUS: *The Wars of the Jews,* Book 1/Chapter 5. 2 (in *The Works of Josephus. Complete and Unabridged,* William Whiston, A. M. translation)

[107] "Peace of Zion"

"*Pharisaism traditionally emphasized humility and the forgiveness of wrongdoing, serving as the guiding principles for the religious group. However, during the civil wars, a significant faction of the Pharisees became politically motivated and adopted a practice of vengeance against their adversaries. They persuaded Queen Salome Alexandra to eliminate all those who had aided Alexander Jannaeus in the crucifixion of the 800 rebellious Pharisees and to prosecute anyone who had assisted him in his persecution of the Pharisees. Subsequently, this faction also orchestrated the downfall of Diogenes, the leader of the Sadducees.*" [108]

Having appointed her elder son Hyrcanus II, as High Priest, she left the command of the army in the hands of her younger son, Aristobulus II.

Open resistance soon emerged among the nobility. A delegation of Sadducees, including Aristobulus II, confronted her regarding the persecution of the Sadducees who had been loyal allies of her late husband and had supported him during times of danger and peril.

Aristobulus II was successful in securing a suspension of the Pharisaic excesses, resulting in a temporary reprieve from armed conflict between the two rival factions.

The Queen granted the Sadducees' request for the right to live outside Jerusalem. She agreed to this arrangement and assigned them the task of guarding various fortresses.

---

[108] *Ant.* 13.16, 2 (410-411)

This decision would later turn out to be a major political blunder. The queen was ultimately unable to prevent Aristobulus II with the Sadducees' assistance from seizing the most important fortresses. This maneuver gave him a significant advantage in the upcoming power struggle against his brother Hyrcanus.

When Alexandra fell sick, Aristobulus II, took hold of this opportunity to take possession of all the fortresses. He also used the sums of money he found in them to get together a number of mercenary soldiers and made himself king.

Before she could punish Aristobulus for his disinheriting his brother, Salome Alexandra died at the age of seventy-three, [109]. She was the last ruler of Yehud to die as a sovereign of an independent kingdom.

Her nine-year reign has been described as a "golden age" of Hasmonean history.

> *Altogether, she managed to keep the Hasmonaean state together. Her reign was one of peace within and without; she increased the army by one half and procured a great body of foreign troops, till her own nation became not only very powerful at home but also terrible to foreign potentates, while she governed other people, and the Pharisees governed her.* [110]

---

[109] 67 B.C.E.

[110] *Wars* I, 5. 2

···

As expected, immediately following her death, civil war broke out between her two sons, Aristobulus II and Hyrcanus II.

Hyrcanus II, as the elder brother, was entitled to the throne and assumed the royal office, having served as High Priest since the beginning of his mother, Salome Alexandra's reign. However, his rule was short-lived, lasting only three months. His younger brother, Aristobulus II, raised an army and ultimately defeated Hyrcanus II in a decisive battle near Jericho.

Following this defeat, Hyrcanus sought refuge in Baris, a fortification established by the Hasmoneans situated on an elevation northwest of the Temple enclosure. In an effort to stabilize the situation, Hyrcanus took Aristobulus's wife and children as hostages. Before the situation escalated further, the two brothers reached an agreement: Hyrcanus would resign, and Aristobulus would ascend to the throne, while Hyrcanus would retain all his other dignities as the king's brother.

"Hereupon they were reconciled to each other in the Temple, and embraced one another in a very kind manner while the people stood round about them." [111]

This, however, did not signal the cessation of the internal struggle for power.

---

[111] JOSEPHUS: *Wars* I, 6.

As Solomon Zeitlin writes, "A brother of a king in the Hellenistic world was a tragic person and always in a precarious position. If he did not raise an army to fight his brother in order to seize power, he was killed by the king to eliminate him as a pretender. Only if the brother was weak or feeble-minded could he hope to live in peace. Hyrcanus was in the latter category." [112]

Hyrcanus II had a wealthy Idumaean friend and advisor named Antipater. His father (also known as Antipater) had been a local commander [113] under Alexander Jannaeus, a title inherited by his son, who evidently wanted to maintain and expand his power by supporting Hyrcanus.

Either because of his friendship with Hyrcanus II, or because he was a descendant of proselytes and believed that the Sadducees (the party that supported Aristobulus) would not allow him to rule Yehud, Antipater hated Aristobulus II.

The Idumean was set to convince Hyrcanus II that his life was in danger because Aristobulus was plotting against him. He pleaded with him to flee to King Aretas in Petra and to request the Nabataean king's support against his brother.

After successfully making arrangements in Nabatea, Antipater and Hyrcanus fled Jerusalem at night and headed for Petra.

---

[112] ZEITLIN, SOLOMON: *The Rise and Fall of the Judaean State. A Political, Social and Religious History of the Second Commonwealth*, Vol I, p. 344
[113] strategos

The price to be paid to the foreign king, a natural enemy of the Hasmonaean kingdom, for assistance in deposing Aristobulus II was the surrender of a large area acquired during the process of restoring the Israelite kingdom, more or less on the model of David's kingdom. This included a number of cities on the eastern side of the Dead Sea, in the old Moabites' territory, which Alexander Jannaeus had taken from the Nabataeans.

Hyrcanus II promised to fulfill this condition. Aretas then marched to Yehud with an army of 50,000 cavalry and infantry and defeated Aristobulus' forces in a battle. Aristobulus was forced to flee to Jerusalem to defend himself in the fortified Temple complex.

The Nabataean king, joined by the Judaeans of Hyrcanus II, then besieged the Temple. Those fighting for Hyrcanus were indirectly facilitating foreign dominance.

By now, the Romans had become increasingly worried at the constant source of instability in Syria under the Seleucids. In 63 B.C.E., Pompey, who had set about the task of remaking the Hellenistic East by creating new client kingdoms and establishing provinces, made Syria a Roman province.

When the Roman general arrived in Damascus, deputations waited upon him from the two brothers and a third from the people itself, begging the abolition of royalty and a restoration of the old priestly constitution. They said that the custom of their country was to obey the priests, and that although the brothers were descendants of priests, they had changed the form of government and enslaved the people. They were willing to live under a foreign government as had their ancestors under Persia, the Ptolemies, and the Seleucids, [114] as long as the government did not interfere with their religious practices.

Antipater, a shrewd politician, marshaled over 1,000 reputable Judaeans from Jerusalem who attested before Pompey to their support for Hyrcanus. Aristobulus, in presenting his case, maintained that Hyrcanus was unfit for the position of king. This had impelled him to assume power; otherwise, there would have been anarchy in the country. Aristobulus, who was attired like a king, presented to Pompey richly dressed young men as witnesses to attest to the truth of his statement.

The Roman general appeared not only as an arbiter between the quarreling brothers but also between them and "the nation," or rather its Pharisaic leadership.[115] He stalled over deciding (allegedly hoping for each side to pay higher bribes) but allowed Aristobulus to accompany him on the expedition against the Nabateans who were besieging Jerusalem.

Suddenly Aristobulus separated from him and fled to the fortress of Alexandrium; he was compelled to surrender the stronghold but managed to escape to Jerusalem. When Pompey appeared before the city, Aristobulus lost heart; he retreated to the Roman camp and offered to deliver the city.

When Gabinius was sent to take over the city, the gates were shut in his face. Pompey, enraged, ordered an advance towards the walls. Though Aristobulus was made

---

[114] *Ant.* 14.3.2 (41)
[115] *Ant.* XIV, 3, 3. 41

prisoner, his followers within the city were determined to defend themselves to the bitter end. They entrenched themselves behind the temple forts.

The siege lasted three months. At last a breach was made in the walls. The Roman soldiers entered, and a terrible massacre ensued. Fully twelve thousand Jews lost their lives.

> *"Pompey, and those that were about him, went into the temple itself whither it was not lawful for any to enter but the high priest, and saw what was reposited therein, the candlestick with its lamps, and the table, and the pouring vessels, and the censers, all made entirely of gold, as also a great quantity of spices heaped together, with two thousand talents of sacred money. Yet he did not touch that money, nor anything else that was there reposited; but he commanded the ministers about the temple, the very next day after he had taken it, to cleanse it and to perform their accustomed sacrifices. Moreover, he made Hyrcanus high priest, [...]"* [116]

Though Pompey himself went into the Holy of Holies, he did not loot or harm the temple itself. But the Hasmonaean kingdom had come to an end. [117]

---

[116] JOSEPHUS, FLAVIUS: *The Wars of the Jews*, Book 1/Chapter 7. 7. (in *The Works of Josephus. Complete and Unabridged*, William Whiston, A. M. translation)

[117] GRABBE, LESTER, L: *An Introduction to First Century Judaism: Jewish Religion and History in the Second Temple Period*, p. 14

Rome tried to rule through the incumbent elite when she first interfered in the province's affairs; thus, Pompey left Hyrcanus II in control of Yehud.

Pompey's annexation brought the independence of the Hasmonean state to an end. Though the Romans had abolished the monarchy, the Hasmoneans continued for another three decades as high priests—under the title "ethnarchs"—but they no longer held political power." [118]

Thus, Roman interventions marked a turning point in Yehud's history, reducing its autonomy and placing it under increasing Roman influence.

Had the Hasmoneans embarked on a concerted and well-coordinated effort, they might have been able to reclaim substantial power—albeit still under Roman oversight—potentially distancing themselves from the influence of Antipater and his sons. Antipater had seized the opportunity, and he strategically positioned his two sons in key governing roles, the elder, Phasael, as governor of Judaea and Herod as governor of Galilee. Both proved to be capable, energetic, and zealous administrators, effectively consolidating their family's influence and authority over the region.

With the fall of the Hasmoneans, the last independent Jewish kingdom came to an end. Their demise was influenced by both internal divisions and external adversaries. The failure of the Hasmoneans to sustain their empire for more than eighty years can be largely attributed to their inability to establish themselves as legitimate and

---

[118] AKENSON, DONALD, HARMAN: *Surpassing Wonder: The Invention of the Bible and the Talmuds*, p. 115

universally recognized leaders, which ultimately contributed to their downfall.

The Third Jewish Commonwealth

Jewish communities have inhabited the Land of Israel for centuries, enduring a prolonged succession of foreign occupations. The Byzantines, Arabs, Seljuk Turks, Crusaders, Mamelukes, and Ottoman Turks were among these occupiers, all of whom repressed and disrupted Jewish life.

Despite this tumultuous history, the descendants of exiled Jews have consistently emigrated to Israel throughout the ages, maintaining a persistent connection to their ancestral homeland. However, it was not until the arrival of Theodor Herzl [119] and the emergence of the Zionist movement that a structured and organized effort to rebuild a Jewish state, truly worthy of its name, began in earnest. Herzl's vision galvanized Jewish communities around the world, fostering a renewed sense of identity and purpose among those who sought to rebuild their sovereign nation in the land of their memories.

The Zionist movement mobilized resources, advocated for political recognition, and encouraged Jewish immigration to what the foreign powers have dubbed Palestine, culminating in the establishment of the State of Israel in 1948. This pivotal moment marked not only the realization of a long-held aspiration but also the beginning of a new chapter in Jewish history—one characterized by both profound challenges and remarkable achievements.

---

[119] d. 1904

In October 1914, Turkey entered the war on Germany's side. One year later, a failed Turkish attempt to attack British posts along the Suez Canal prompted His Majesty's Forces to recognize the land of Yehud as a strategic asset. This territory was not merely a crucial stepping-stone to the Suez Canal; it also constituted an integral part of the overland route to India, which traversed through Egypt, Transjordan, Iraq, and the Persian Gulf. India was widely regarded as the jewel in the crown of the British Empire, and therefore, the control of these routes was deemed essential to British imperial interests.

On December 11, 1917, on the eve of the holiday of Hanukkah, British General Sir Edmund Allenby entered Jerusalem, putting an end to more than seven hundred years of Muslim occupation of the land of Yehud. This momentous event symbolized not only a shift in control over a city of profound historical and religious significance but also heralded a new chapter in the Zionist movement's aspirations for a Jewish homeland.

• • •

"It is a boy!" exclaimed Mark Sykes, a prominent British diplomat, on opening the doors where the British war cabinet was meeting into the anteroom where Chaim Weizmann, Israel's future first president, was anxiously waiting.

The "boy" in question was the Balfour Declaration, the landmark pronouncement [120] by which Britain committed

---

[120] November 2, 1917

itself to support the establishment of a Jewish homeland in the land of Yehud.

Balfour was the acknowledgment from one of the world's major powers of the Jewish people's right to establish a nation in their ancestral land, setting in motion a series of events that would ultimately lead to the founding of the State of Israel.

Under the British caretaker government, during the 1930s and 1940s, the Jewish community in Yehud was dominated by an intense internal conflict between the two major political movements, the Socialists and the Revisionists.

The infighting that tore apart the Zionist movement in the pre-state era was so fierce that the left-wing underground Palmach militia once kidnapped members of the right-wing underground Irgun and handed them over to the British occupiers. In 1948, during Israel's War of Independence, Labor Prime Minister David Ben-Gurion directed the IDF to sink an Irgun ship loaded with arms and Jewish volunteers off the coast of Tel Aviv; this, despite the fact that the ship was flying a white flag, 16 Jewish members of the Irgun were killed.

The British had initially entered Yehud with the objective of defeating the Turks; however, they had remained in the region to prevent French influence from taking hold. Then, on May 14, 1948, they abruptly relinquished control over Yehud, almost slamming the door behind them, leaving the Zionist leadership to navigate the tumultuous waters of statehood amidst their internal discord.

· · ·

At 4 P.M. in a hall in the Tel Aviv Museum, where paintings by Marc Chagall's *A Jew Holding a Scroll of the Law*, Maurycy Minkowski's Pogroms, Shmuel Hirshenberg's *Exile*, and a large portrait of Herzl [121], flanked by blue and white flags, had been freshly hung, the now sixty-two-year-old David Ben Gurion, Prime Minister of the State of Israel in waiting, read aloud the "Scroll of the Establishment of the State of Israel." [122]

Israel's Declaration of Independence stipulated that a constitution would be established "not later than the first day of October, 1948."

It never happened.

The document that could have potentially healed the rifts in Israeli society and served as a central component of the state's identity remained an impossibility, the differences of opinion were so profound that reconciliation seemed unattainable.

At the ninth session of the Provisional State Council in July 1949, Meir David Levinstein spoke on behalf of the Haredi Agudat Israel party and declared that a constitution would be rejected under any circumstances. "It must be understood," he said, "that a secular constitution will be boycotted by Torah-true Jews, not only in our state but throughout the lands of the Diaspora."

---

[121] The father of political Zionism
[122] MORRIS, BENNY: 1948: *A History of the First Arab- Israeli War*, p. 178

"A constitution is not enacted; it is granted; it is granted by the Almighty," added Zerah Wahrhaftig, leader of Mizrahi, another Orthodox religious party.

The *"datim,"*[123] however, were not the only ones opposed to enacting a constitution for the newly refounded Jewish State. Prime Minister David Ben-Gurion argued that it would be a mistake to rush into a constricting legal straitjacket.

As Israeli historian Anita Shapira explains: [124]

The Israeli legislators reviewed the model of the American Constitution, which grants the Supreme Court the power to declare laws passed by the legislative branch unconstitutional. To Ben-Gurion, this authority seemed to bypass the wishes of the democratic majority and restrict the government's decision-making power.

For precisely the same reason, the parties at both ends of the political spectrum—Mapam (United Workers Party) and Herut ("liberty," the main right-wing party)—supported a constitution, since it would protect individual and minority rights against the coercive power of the majority. They feared that without a constitution, a government headed by Mapai could enact laws damaging to the small parties.

• • •

---

[123] In modern Israel a general name for religious Jews
[124] SHAPIRA, ANITA: *Israel: A History* (Kindle loc. 4087)

On the day after Israel declared its independence, five armies, alongside the remnants of the Arab Legion and the Transjordan Frontier Force, mobilized to challenge the nascent state's existence. These forces included contingents from Egypt, bolstered by a unit of the Saudi Arabian army, as well as troops from Jordan, Lebanon, Syria, and Iraq. Their collective objective was to disrupt Israel's statehood through a concerted military campaign aimed at overturning the establishment of the new nation.

The civilian population of the nascent State of Israel, organized in its totality as a militia, found itself confronting professional Arab armies in the north, center, and south of the newly independent country. As in Maccabean times, the same commitment to life, the genius and organizational capacity of its planners, the faith, and the courage up to the last echelon of the social pyramid combined to beat the odds and the superiority of numbers. The invading armies were defeated.

On February 24, 1949, Egypt signed an armistice agreement with Israel, confirming Israeli control over the Negev. A month later, the Israeli forces withdrew from the area held in Lebanon in accordance with the agreement reached with that country following the Egyptian armistice. On April 3, 1949, an armistice agreement was reached with Jordan, and a final one was reached with Syria on July 20, 1949.

The War of Independence was over, and the State of Israel was established within the borders delineated by the armistice agreements.

These agreements were originally intended to serve as preliminary steps toward a peace treaty, which was to be signed within a six-month timeframe. However, the process dragged on for several years, ultimately leading to the lapsing of agreements.

All compromise proposals for peace put forth by the Israelis over the years were categorically rejected by the Arab nations, primarily because they refused to acknowledge the legitimacy of the Jewish State's existence back in their homeland in the lands that the Arabs had occupied.

• • •

Seven years after having signed the armistice with Egypt, Israel went to war again with its foe in the south in an effort to restrain the persistent raids conducted by fedayeen guerrillas originating from Gaza.

The 1956 "Sinai War" was originally intended as a coordinated campaign involving British and French forces. Both countries sought to reclaim control over the Suez Canal, the vital waterway that had been nationalized by Egyptian President Gamal Abdel Nasser.

The geopolitical landscape of the time was heavily influenced by Cold War dynamics, and as the conflict escalated, the United States exerted considerable pressure on both Britain and France.

Faced with mounting international condemnation and the prospect of strained relations with the United States, the

British and French forces withdrew from the conflict and quickly distanced themselves from the Israeli actions.

By February 1957, the situation reached a critical stage. Under substantial pressure from both American and Soviet authorities, Israel was compelled to withdraw from the territories it had occupied and revert to its pre-war boundaries.

However, the newly established Jewish state did derive some strategic advantage from this conflict: a deployment of a United Nations peacekeeping force along the Gaza border. This presence largely contributed to the cessation of the *fedayeen* raids that had previously plagued them.

• • •

Ten years later, Egyptian President Gamal Abdel Nasser, breaching the accord to keep the Sinai demilitarized, ordered the withdrawal of United Nations peacekeepers from the region and closed the Straits of Tiran, Israel's vital gateway to the Red Sea.

This ominous provocation heightened tensions throughout the region, with Syria, Iraq, and Jordan all preparing for war.

In response to the impending threat, Israel launched a preemptive strike, motivated solely by the urgent desire to avoid destruction.

Defense Minister Moshe Dayan spoke to Israel's soldiers as they prepared for battle,

> *"We have no aim of conquest. Our sole objectives are to put an end to the Arab attempt to conquer our land and to suppress the blockade and the belligerence mounted against us. ... We are a small but brave people. We want peace, but we are ready to fight for our land and our lives."*

General Yitzhak Rabin, head of the IDF, and his staff devised a strategic operational plan to conquer Gaza and use it as a bargaining chip to persuade Egypt to reopen the Straits of Tiran. It was a tactical strategy aimed at securing Israel's borders and protecting its citizens.

General Israel Tal, commander of the armored division, issued a proclamation:

> *" "This is a battle that the enemy wanted and the enemy began; we will strike the enemy twice as hard as he hit us. ... For the third time, the Egyptian dagger has been brandished at us. For the third time, the enemy has erred in its mad delusion of seeing Israel brought to its knees. With blood, fire, and iron, this time we shall purge this plot from their heart... We do not covet their land or their property. We have not come to destroy their country nor to take possession of it."*

Nasser had succeeded in one thing: frightening Israel. [125]

[125] GORENBERG, GERSHOM: *The Accidental Empire. Israel and the Birth of the Settlements*, 1967- 1977, p. 34

At 7:10 a.m. on Monday, June 5, 1967, dozens of Mirages and Mystères warplanes began taking off from Tel Nof airbase near Tel Aviv and headed south. The planes were flying so low over the trees that it felt as if one could lift his hand and touch their wings. For the next ninety minutes, planes took off and returned and took off again." [126]

Throughout most of the day, Nasser studied the transmitted reports of Egyptian "victories." None of his commanders gave him the actual facts. It was only at 4:00 p.m. that a headquarters officer arrived with straight information: "I have come to tell you that we no longer have an air force."

Israel's military planning and strategy, including the initial commitment of the entire Israel Air Force to the southern front on the morning of June 5, were geared toward the hope that the war would be limited to Egypt. But IDF planning also had considered the possible entry of Jordan and Syria into the war.

Prime Minister Levi Eshkol had transmitted an urgent message to Jordan's King Hussein:

> "We are engaged in a defensive battle in the Egyptian sector, and we will initiate no action in the Jerusalem sector unless Jordan attacks us. If Jordan attacks Israel, we will assault her with all our forces."

King Hussein later acknowledged that

---

[126] HALEVI, YOSSI KLEIN: *Like Dreamers: The Story of the Israeli Paratroopers Who Reunited Jerusalem and Divided a Nation*, p. 68

"Israel had warned that if we did not intervene, they would save us from consequences that otherwise were inevitable, but by that time we no longer had any choice. We were obliged to do everything to help our allies," the king said.

Once the lines had been crossed and the area occupied, the war's objectives shifted from defensive to liberation.

With seven brigades under his command known as Central Command, Major General Uzi Narkiss was responsible for combating any possible Jordanian offensive. Capturing the Old City was not part of the plan. However, Narkiss, who had fought in the failed battle for the Old City of Jerusalem in 1948, had his own unfinished business and wanted to exploit any Jordanian attack to take the West Bank.

At 10 a.m. on Monday, June 5, 1967, Jordanian army howitzers launched the first of 6,000 shells on Jewish Jerusalem, beginning with Kibbutz Ramat Rachel in the south and Mount Scopus in the north. The shelling continued for the next ten hours, killing twenty civilians, including two children, and injuring over one thousand people. Over 900 buildings would be damaged, including hospitals, schools, the Israel Museum, the president's home, the Knesset building, and the house next door to Prime Minister Levi Eshkol. A few stores burned down. In the Biblical Zoo, some ninety animals died. There was heavy damage to streets, and trees were burned.

Despite his instincts to strike back quickly, Narkiss remained under orders to hold tight unless a major Jordanian invasion attempt were launched. Even when

Arab shelling grew heavier, Defense Minister Moshe Dayan's instructions to the central front commander were to "grit your teeth and don't ask for more troops from GHQ." [127]

At noon on Tuesday, June 6, Dayan arrived by helicopter in West Jerusalem. Narkiss met him and drove him to Mt. Scopus in a Jeep through a stretch of land captured before dawn that morning. The view from the vantage point is spectacular; the Dome of the Rock appears to be within reach.

Narkiss said, "Moshe, we have to go into the Old City."

Dayan replied, "Absolutely not." Surround the walled city from the east, he told Narkiss, but keep clear of "all that Vatican."

The fact is, Dayan also wanted to conquer the Old City, but without damaging the holy places there, without risking diplomatic fallout. [128]

On Wednesday, June 7, Menachem Begin and Prime Minister Eshkol, expecting an imminent U.N. ceasefire, called Dayan. At seven o'clock that morning, the defense minister entered the war room and finally issued the order for Jerusalem's Old City to be occupied as quickly as possible.

---

[127] SACHAR, M. HOWARD.: *A History of Israel. From the Rise of Zionism to Our Time*, p. 644
[128] GORENBERG, GERSHOM: *The End of Days. Fundamentalism and the Struggle for the Temple Mount*, pp. 98- 99

At 10:00 a.m. Colonel Mordechai "Motta" Gur, commanding the 55th Paratroopers Reserve Brigade that entered the Old City of Jerusalem, announced,

> *"The Temple Mount is ours!"*

General Narkiss expressed what was in everybody's mind at the time.

> *"Jerusalem has been conquered or overrun thirty-seven times.*
>
> *In June, 1967, we liberated our city for what we hope will be the last time and for what we pray will be the first generation of its complete redemption."* [129]

• • •

On Israel's Independence Day, 24 days earlier, Rabbi Tzvi Yehudah Hacohen Kook, the head of the "Merkaz ha-Rav Yeshiva," in Jerusalem, was delivering his annual Israel's Independence Day sermon when he suddenly interrupted himself with a sobbing scream:

> *"Where is our Hebron, Shechem, Jericho, and Anathoth [130] torn from the state in 1948 as we lay maimed and bleeding?"*

---

[129] NARKISS, UZI: *The Liberation of Jerusalem: The Battle of 1967*, p. 258
[130] historical sites sacred to Judaism]

The abruptness and form of the exclamation did not appear to be part of the sermon; rather, it was a spontaneous release from the depths of the mind. Even so, the message was clear: the partition of the Land of Israel orchestrated by foreign powers was intolerable.

Three weeks following the sermon. The land was conquered, and the ancient cities whose names the rabbi had proclaimed became a reality. His students declared their teacher's Independence Day sermon to be a prophecy.

On June 7, Rabbi Zvi Yehuda's students, who were among the first soldiers to reach the Western Wall of the destroyed Temple, asked their commander, Motta Gur, to send a military jeep to bring the rabbi to the wall. Upon arrival, Rabbi Kook declared:

> *"We hereby inform the people of Israel and the entire world that under heavenly command we have just returned home in the elevations of holiness and our holy city. We shall never move out of here."* [131]

Later, from the pulpit, the rabbi explained the significance of what had just happened:

> *'We have to see the greatness of this hour in its biblical dimension, and it can be seen only through the messianic perspective…only in the light of the Messiah."*

Religious messianism had now become political messianism. The roadmap of redemption was now in

---

[131] Quoted in S. Daniel, "You First Build on Sand and Then Proceed to Sanctify," *Hatzofe*, Iyar 23, 1973

human hands. And the driver was the National Religious Party.

• • •

Once again, on the afternoon of October 6, 1973, Prime Minister Golda. Meir addressed the country on television and radio:

> *Citizens of Israel: At around 14:00 today, the armies of Egypt and Syria launched an offensive against Israel... The Israel Defense Forces are fighting back and repulsing the attack. The enemy has suffered serious losses... They hoped to surprise the citizens of Israel on the Day of Atonement while many were praying in the synagogues... But we are not surprised... Our forces were deployed as necessary to meet the danger. We have no doubt about our victory, but we consider the resumption of the Egyptian-Syrian aggression as tantamount to an act of madness."[132]*

Also known as the Yom Kippur War, it was the fourth major military confrontation between Israel and the Arab states since 1948.

> *"No one dared to doubt this time that we were under threat of annihilation. This was no normal international dispute, no quarrel about borders. It required no special gift for making historical*

---

[132] SACHAR, M. HOWARD: *A History of Israel: From the Rise of Zionism to Our Time*, p. 763

analogies to see that in the joint onslaught on Israel
made by the Arab armies and their helpers from a
dozen lands, there was a genocidal intent, a
continuation of Hitler's war against the Jewish
people. The issue was not this or that piece of land;
the issue was Israel's right to national existence,
the Jewish people's right to physical space. But
there was a metaphysical dimension also. The war
was launched on Yom Kippur because it was
thought that on that day the frontline soldiers would
be less on the alert than on other days of the year—
this was an important tactical consideration." [133]

Despite the element of surprise and the bitter defeats
suffered in the early days of combat, the Yom Kippur War
ended with a major Israeli victory.

However, the Israeli public did not see it this way.

The leadership, represented mainly by the Israeli Labor
Party, which had played a pivotal role in national decision-
making since 1933, had irrevocably lost the trust of the
people. As a result of the collective grief over the
thousands of soldiers who had died and the injured
civilians, the country had entered a state of national trauma
whose effects would last for decades.

• • •

In the 1973 elections, which occurred just two months after
the Yom Kippur War, Menachem Begin, the leader of the

---

[133] FISCH, HAROLD: *The Zionist Revolution: A New Perspective*, p. 91

right-wing political party, aligned himself with a strategy proposed by retired General Ariel Sharon, who was widely regarded as a hero of the recent conflict. Together, they sought to consolidate a larger bloc of opposition parties against Labor, which had maintained a dominant position in Israeli governance since the country's establishment.

This coalition was established under the name of Likud. [134]

The formation of Likud signaled a significant shift in Israeli political dynamics; right-wing forces had consolidated to challenge the Labor Party's long-held hegemony. The formation of this coalition not only reflected the shifting sentiments of the Israeli electorate in the aftermath of the Yom Kippur War, but it also reshaped the political landscape.

Most Zionist Israelis, traumatized by the Second Intifada's suicide bombings and discouraged from territorial compromise by the rise of Hezbollah and Hamas terror forces in the territories from which they withdrew, rejected the Israeli left's land for peace concept as a failed experiment.

Many Mizrahim Israelis, primarily first- and second-generation Jewish refugees from Arab countries, were drawn to Begin because they saw the current political establishment as treating them as second-class citizens. His open support for Judaism stood in stark contrast to the Labor Alignment's secularism, which alienated many Mizrahi voters. This ideological divide enabled Begin to build a strong political base among the Mizrahi

---

[134] Likud means in Hebrew "Consolidation."

community, which was captivated by his vision and rhetoric.

On June 19, 1977, Likud formalized a coalition agreement with the National Religious Party, which held twelve seats, as well as with the Agudat Yisrael party. Following eight hours of debate, Begin's government was officially approved in a Knesset vote on June 21, 1977, thereby making him the new Prime Minister of Israel.

The country had elected as its leader the man who, on the campaign trail, had said that "between the Mediterranean Sea and the Jordan River, there shall only be Israeli sovereignty."

• • •

Time after time, Jewish religious messianists have attempted to burst into Haram al-Sharif/Temple Mount to establish Israeli sovereignty there and build the Third Temple.

Their argument had been that the main issue is not prayers but sovereignty. Control, ownership, authority. Because what is the point of defining the state as Jewish if it has agreed to share the place most sacred to its believers with the Muslims? And that is not the only contradiction caused by the religious state. The Temple Mount is located in an area that Israel has annexed." [135]

---

[135] BAR'EL, ZVI: "A War Over the Temple Mount Is Just a Matter of Time," "Haaretz," Apr 19, 2022

Begin extended an invitation to Moshe Dayan to serve as his minister of foreign affairs, Dayan had to contend with Sheik Azzam al-Khatib's contention that "this place belongs to the Muslim people, and no others have the right to pray here. If they try to take over the mosque, this will be the end of time."

Al-Khatib, the director of the Waqf, the Islamic trust that administers the site, had said that the mosque was a unifying symbol for the world's 1.2 billion Muslims and warned, "This will create rage and anger not only in the West Bank but all over the Islamic world—and only God knows what will happen." [136]

Dayan reaffirmed the ruling, known as the Temple Mount's status quo, he gave in 1967, by which Muslims will pray at the Al-Aqsa Mosque and the Dome of the Rock, and Jews at the Western Wall, the portion of the Second Temple's retaining wall that remains today. He further determined that Jews would be permitted to visit the Temple Mount solely as tourists, not as worshipers.

Still, since 1967, approximately 27 organizations affiliated with the "Joint Committee of Temple Organizations" have regarded each day as a missed opportunity to commence the construction of the Third Temple. [137]

Why, the fundamentalists ask, should Jews consider the Western Wall, which is nothing but the remains of the outer courtyard of Herod's Temple, a particularly holy

---

[136] BOOTH, WILLIAM and EGLASH, RUTH: "Jewish activists want to pray on Jerusalem's Temple Mount, raising alarm in Muslim world," "The Washington Post," December 2, 2013
[137] For many conservative Christians around the world, notably in the United States, constructing the temple is a prerequisite for the Second Coming.

place? What sort of authentic redemptionist Zionism is it whose adherents stand at the Western Wall and hypocritically commemorate the Temple's destruction by fasting and bemoaning the plight of Jews "unable" to "return to the Mountain of the Lord and rebuild the Temple"?"[138]

In countering that argument, some Israeli thinkers, such as journalist and historian Gershom Gorenberg, likely having the Hasmonean period experience back in their mind, pose the question:

"Why isn't the Western Wall sufficient as a Jewish center? The Wall already demonstrates that nothing can divide Jews like a central holy location; the Orthodox state Rabbinate that governs the site prohibits other Jewish denominations, such as Conservative and Reform, from performing ceremonies there. Adding a temple would only exacerbate the problem." [139]

• • •

Seventy-five years after Ben-Gurion opposed establishing a constitution, the unresolved issues dividing the citizens of the third Jewish Commonwealth resurfaced, erupting with vengeance.

For months, beginning in 2023, hundreds of thousands of Israelis protested in the streets of Israel's largest cities

---

[138] LUSTICK, IAN, S.: "Israel's Dangerous Fundamentalists," "Foreign Policy," Number 68, Fall 1987
[139] GORENBERG, GERSHOM: *The End of Days. Fundamentalism and the Struggle for the Temple Mount*, pp. 67- 68

against the intended policies of Israel's 37th government, [140] to effect a profound judicial reform, basically arguing what was argued in Ben-Gurion's time:

That the Supreme Court overstepped its authority (due in large part to the absence of a Constitution), ignored the wishes of the democratic majority, and limited the government's decision-making authority. The opposition, on the other hand, contended that lifting the Supreme Court's protective shield would expose individual and minority rights to the majority's coercive powers.

But, ultimately, the dividing issue was the same one that plagued the Hasmoneans and resulted in the destruction of the second Jewish Commonwealth, namely:

What kind of society do the Jews want to live in?

Tzipi Livni, who served in the cabinets of right-wing Prime Ministers Ariel Sharon and Ehud Olmert before switching to the center, explained the choice.

> *"The split is between those that believe Israel should be a more religious country with less democracy and see democracy as only a system of elections and not a set of values, and those who want Israel to remain a Jewish and democratic state."*

More than ever, Israelis view each other as members of ideological, religious, or ethnic sub-units, rather than as one society with shared values.

---

[140] Formed on December 29, 2022

● ● ●

In 2015, Reuven Rivlin, Israel's tenth president, noted that children born in the State of Israel are assigned to one of four unique educational systems. Each of these systems is designed to educate the child and shape their worldview based on a different ethos or culture, religious belief, or even national identity.

A child from a religious settler town like Beth El, a Bedouin Arab child from Rahat, a secular Jewish child from Herzliya, and a Haredi child from Beitar Ilit not only do not meet, but they are also educated to have completely different perspectives on the fundamental values and desired character of Israel.

In addition to their own town and school system, each tribe—the secular, the national-religious, the Haredi, and the Arab—as President Rivlin referred to these various groups, has its own media platform, the newspapers they read, and the television channels they watch.

● ● ●

Jews have never been of a single mind. Israel began as a confederation of tribes. Not long after the tribes united under a monarchical system, they separated into two separate kingdoms: Judah and Israel. Then Hellenizers and zealots, Samaritans and Pharisees, Jews and Christians, Rabbinites and Karaites, Liberals and Orthodox, Zionists and Anti-Zionists.

In discussing the phenomena of Jewish divisiveness, my teacher, the late Jacob B. Agus, would say:

> *We may employ the slogan "We are one," providing we understand that we are also many and diverse. We are one, as a family of religious and national communities, a family of adults who are mature enough to go their separate ways and loyal enough to their common tradition to feel that they form "one fellowship."*

The Jewish people to this day remain a unity, but they are not unanimous. Rather than serving as a common glue, Judaism has become the source of divisiveness among Jews.

Israeli cultural politics need not be a zero-sum game, imposing the values of one community over others.

In what relates to Israel, the Swiss model—a federation of 26 cantons—and the Canadian provincial system come up repetitively.

Swiss democracy, for instance, is not a majority democracy where there are winners and losers. Everyone is part of the government, not only in parliament. In Switzerland, all the population groups take part in decision-making, and one group cannot completely ignore the opinions, rights, or feelings of others. The different groups have veto power, irrespective of their size. [141]

---

[141] MASHIACH, ITAY: "A Federation, Cantons, Autonomous Regions? Suddenly Everyone Is Talking About Dividing Israel," "Haaretz," May 5, 2023

In 2014, journalist Judd Yadid and the late psychologist and philosopher Carlo Strenger draw a comprehensive federalist map aimed at maintaining national unity in Israel while simultaneously enabling the expression of the country's diverse identities.

The proposal included detailed ideas for the establishment of an Orthodox religious province that would encompass the majority of the nation's religious Jews, ensuring that they have the highest possible degree of cultural autonomy. This province would extend from Jerusalem's northwest corner to Beit Shemesh, Modi'in, and Bnei Brak.

The greater Tel Aviv province, which is the sum of the current Tel Aviv District minus Bnei Brak and Petah Tikva, would be situated at the opposite end of the spectrum.

By redrawing the Northern and Southern Districts, minority land rights would be safeguarded, and a continuous chain of Jewish-majority provinces that spans the entire country would be established.

A little bit tongue-in-cheek. Dr. Strenger wrote:

As in Switzerland and the United States, most of the taxes will go to the states that make up the republic rather than to the federal government. Let the ultra-Orthodox argue among themselves about whether they want to keep men and women apart on the bus. Let them have kosher cell phones and teach their children nothing but Jewish subjects. Let them also figure out how they will fund their state.

In the state of Judea, let Zionist right-wingers argue about whether women can sing at public events, whether children should be taught that Shimon Bar Kochba was a hero, and whether King David should be the ideal role model for future leaders. If they want, they can turn their state into a kingdom, which is what a growing number of religious Zionist rabbis want anyway."[142]

Proponents of cantonization contend that Israel should and can achieve a similar level of autonomy in various domains, including education, health, and personal status (including marriage), as the Swiss cantons do.

• • •

It is a truism that one cannot reach a destination if he does not know where he is going. Jews know where they are going; they just disagree on how to get there.

Jews know where they are going because Judaism is a goal-oriented culture.

It has made as its concern the response-ability of each individual Jew to the challenges, stumbling blocks, questions, and accomplishments confronting them.

The enemies of the Jews get it right. The head of Hizballah, the terror organization based in Lebanon that has brought so much havoc and death around the world, for instance, stated, 'The Jews love life, so that is what we shall

[142] STRENGER, CARLO: "Give Israel's secular liberals their own state," "Ha'aretz," January 9, 2012

take away from them. We are going to win because they love life, and we love death."

He was right in his premise; he was wrong in his conclusion. As there have been all of those who, through time, have invested their efforts in trying to destroy the Jews.

The goal of Judaism for its people had been enunciated over twenty-six hundred years ago in the Torah.

"Choose life." [143]

Not country, nor religion, nor an idea, which are no more than instruments for humans to live, not to die.

The whole biblical verse reads:

"I call heaven and earth as witnesses! Before you, I have placed life and death, the blessing and the curse. You must choose life so that you and your descendants will survive."

---

[143] *Deut.* 30: 19: "*You must choose life so that you and your descendants will survive.*"

Appendix

Antioch on the Orontes. The capital of the Seleucid Empire. Founded by Seleucus I Nicator, one of Alexander the Great's generals. Situated in what is today the Hatay province of southern Turkey in the Syrian border with Turkey.

Coele-Syria. Antiochus III renamed the conquered Ptolemaic province of Syria and Phoenicia "Coele-Syria and Phoenicia," frequently abbreviated to 'Coele-Syria.'

Hasidim. These were the *Hasidim harishonim* (the *early pietists*) of the second century B.C.E.; not to be confused with the Jewish religious movement that began in the 18th century in Eastern Europe and is extant today. According to Rabbi Jacob B. Agus, they were the "spiritual athletes," out of which there diverged in later years the Essenes, the Therapeutae of Philo, the sectarians of the found Dead Sea Scrolls, and the Pharisees."[144]

They are briefly mentioned three times in the classical sources (*1 Macc.* 2: 41; *1 Macc.* 7: 14; and *2 Macc. 14:6).* The Book of Jubilees can be identified as a Hasidic writing since it contains historical allusions to Maccabean victories down to the years 163 or perhaps 161 B.C.E. The War

---

[144] AGUS, J.B.: The Vision and the Way, p. 77

Scroll from Cave 11, among the Dead Sea Scrolls, can also be identified as a Hasidic composition.

They joined forces with the Maccabees, furnishing the rank and file of the warriors, and their enthusiasm helped carry the revolt through many reverses to final victory. . When the Hasmoneans became the new rulers and followed the footsteps of the Seleucids, exalting the state above all else, the Pharisees denounced them as enemies of Judaism. There is some ground for the supposition that the sect was first organized under Simon the Just at the beginning of the second century B.C.E.

The Hasidim were the chief scribes and authoritative interpreters of the regulations and commandments of the Torah."[145]

They are also described as the "orthodox" Jews who opposed the "Hellenizers" under the Hellenistic reform of Jason and Menelaus. [146]

Simon the Just himself belonged, apparently, to the Hasidim, and, as he was chief and leader of the theocratic commonwealth, the scribal interpretations were accepted by the priesthood, and the Oral Law fostered by the scribes was declared by the Jerusalem community to be the official authoritative interpretation of the Mosaic Law. [147]

Though they were the main military supporters of Judah Maccabee from 166 to 162 B.C.E., they had already gained

[145] TCHERIKOVER, V.: Hellenistic Civilization and the Jews, p. 197
[146] GRABBE, LESTER, L.: Judaism from Cyrus to Hadrian, Vol. II, p. 466
[147] TCHERIKOVER, VICTOR: Hellenistic Civilization and the Jews, p. 125

a reputation as "mighty warriors of Israel" before they placed themselves under his command.

Their conflict with the Hellenists manifested itself primarily in the struggle for control of the high priesthood. Their religious and political objectives coincided with that of Onias III and his priestly supporters. [148]

"They were extremists, and they arose as a reaction to the other extremists who were willing to give up Judaism for Hellenism. As extremists, the Hasidim sought only to save their own souls and were not interested in saving the Law for the Judeans as a people." [149]

"The Jewish temple and ancestral religion had been restored in 164 BCE, and the wicked high priest Menelaus had been executed in 162 BCE. Onias IV, the last of the Oniads in Judea, took refuge in Egypt that same year. Little reason remained for the Hasidim to exist as a social movement or formal community. In 162 BCE, leading Hasidim were prepared to abandon Judas Maccabaeus and negotiate for peace with the Seleucids. After this date, the Hasidim are not heard of again." [150]

Gerousia. "From the Restoration (516 B.C.E.) till the Hasmonean Revolt (165 B.C.E.), Yehud was a theocracy.

---

[148] GMIRKIN, RUSSEL: The War Scroll, the Hasidim, and the Maccabean Conflict," http://cojs.org/the_war_scroll-_the_hasidim-_and_the_maccabean_conflict-_russel_gmirkin/
[149] ZEITLIN, SOLOMON: The Rise and Fall of the Judaean State. A Political, Social and Religious History of the Second Commonwealth, Vol I., p. 91
[150] GMIRKIN, RUSSEL: The War Scroll, the Hasidim, and the Maccabean Conflict," http://cojs.org/the_war_scroll-_the_hasidim-_and_the_maccabean_conflict-_russel_gmirkin/

The high priest at its head was assisted by the Gerousia. This aristocratic body was a supreme council and tribunal, composed of priestly and lay elders (*zekenim* in Hebrew). Though the members were not elected, they were appointed through some form of popular sanction. This Judean institution was vested with full power (*Ant*. 12.3.3 (138), as shown in the Book of Judith (*Judith* 4: 8; 11, 14). However, "the influence of the gerousia varied inversely with the strength of the high priest. When Simon, the last of the Hasmonean brothers, became ruler of the Jewish state by acclaim of the people (*I Macc.* 14: 28), a new form of government finally came into existence, and the old gerousia disappeared, not to be recorded any more." [151]

It evolved into the Sanhedrin.

Pharisees. The Hasmonean period was dominated by the conflict between the Sadducees and Pharisees, who took turns contending for and exercising ascendancy.The name was coined and used by the Sadducees, who resented the reforms and the new laws that were adopted by Ezra and his associates. The disciples of Ezra, who called themselves Hasidim and ultimately were nicknamed *Perushim*, Pharisees—had separated themselves from the people of the land, the people of Yehud, the Jews. Thus the name *Perushim* was a nickname of reproach and contempt.

Pharisaism became Talmudism, Talmudism became Medieval Rabbinism, and Medieval Rabbinism became Modern Rabbinism. Orthodoxy has equated itself with Pharisaism since the beginning of time, and Reform

---

[151] HOENIG, SIDNEY, B.: The Great Sanhedrin: A Study of the Origin, Development, Composition and Functions of the *Bet Din ha-Gadol* during the Second Jewish Commonwealth, p. 12

Judaism also recognizes a progressive, democratic current in the Jewish religion of the Second Commonwealth in that movement. [152]

Sadducees. Sadducism was the product of the Temple hierarchy and the provincial aristocracy. With the only exception of Salome Alexandra's reign (76-67 B.C.E.), they were constantly associated with Judean political and religious power all through the late Second Temple period. The emergence of this party can be traced to the time of Ezra the Scribe. At that time, he and his associates on their return from Babylon attempted to interpret the Torah in accordance with the tradition of the elders. By doing this, they aroused the opposition of the Zadok family, who monopolized the Temple and the leadership over the Jews. The Zadokites—or Sadducees—strongly contested the ideas of Ezra and his associates. [153]

[152] BARON, SALO WITTMAYER: A Social and Religious History of the Jews, Vol. II, p. 344
[153] ZEITLIN, SOLOMON: Studies in the Early History of Judaism, Vol. II, p. 261

Bibliography

ACKOYD, PETER, R.: *Exile and Restoration: A Study of Hebrew Thought of the Sixth Century B.C.* Philadelphia. The Westminster Press. 1968.

AGUS, J.B.: *The Meaning of Jewish History.* Vol. I. USA. Abelard- Schuman. 1963.

AHARONI, YOHANAN: *The Land of the Bible: A Historical Geography.* Philadelphia: The Westminster Press. (c. 1962). 2nd ed. 1979.

AKENSON, DONALD HARMAN: *Surpassing Wonder: The Invention of the Bible and the Talmuds.* Chicago: The University of Chicago Press. 2001.

ALBERTZ, RAINER: *Israel in Exile: The History and Literature of the Sixth Century B.C.E.* Atlanta: Society of Biblical Literature, 2003.

ASSMAN, JAN: *Religion and Cultural Memory: Ten Studies.* Stanford: Stanford University Press. 2006

AVI-YONAH, MICHAEL: *The Jews of Palestine: A Political History from the Bar Kokba War to the Arab Conquest.* New York. Schocken Books, 1976.

AVI-YONAH, MICHAEL: *The Jews Under Roman and Byzantine Rule.* New York: Schocken Books/Magnes Press, 1984.

BARON, SALO, WITTMAYER: *A Social and Religious History of the Jews.* Vol. I. Philadelphia. Philadelphia: The Jewish Publication Society of America, 1952.

BIALE, DAVID: *Power & Powerlessness in Jewish History.* New York: Schocken Books, 1986.

BICKERMAN, ELIAS: *From Ezra to the Last of the Maccabees.* New York: Schocken Books. (1949) 2nd. 1966.

151

BICKERMAN, ELIAS, J.: *The Jews in the Greek Age*. Cambridge, Massachusetts: Harvard University Press. 1988.

BLENKINSOPP, JOSEPH: *Judaism: The First Phase. The Place of Ezra and Nehemiah in the Origins of Judaism*. Grand Rapids, Michigan. William B. Eerdmans Publishing Company. 2009.

BOCCACCINI, GABRIELE: *Roots of Rabbinic Judaism: An Intellectual History, from Ezekiel to Daniel*. William B. Eerdmann Publishing Company. Grand Rapids, Michigan/Cambridge, U.K. 2002, 226 pages.

CLINE, ERIC, H.: *Jerusalem Besieged: From Ancient Canaan to Modern Israel*. Ann Arbor: The University of Michigan Press, 2004.

COHEN, SHAYE, J.D.: *From the Maccabees to the Mishnah*. Louisville, London, Westminster: Yohanan Knox Press, 2006 [2nd, 1st 1989].

DAVIES, PHILIP, R.: *Memories of Ancient Israel: An Introduction to Biblical History—Ancient and Modern*. Louisville, London, Westminster: Yohanan Knox Press. 2008.

FACKENHEIM, EMIL, L.: *Encounters Between Judaism and Modern Philosophy. A preface to Future Jewish Thought*. New York: Schocken Books. 1980 [1st. 1973].

GERA, DOV: *Judaea and Mediterranean Politics 219 to 161 B.C.E.* Leiden. New York. Koln: Brill. 1998.

GILBERT, MARTIN: *Exile and Return: The Emergence of Jewish Statehood*. London: Weinfeld and Nicolson. 1978.

GOODMAN, MARTIN: *The Ruling Class of Judaea: The Origins of the Jewish Revolt Against Rome A.D. 66-70*. New York: Cambridge University Press. 1993.

GORENBERG, GERSHOM: *The End of Days: Fundamentalism and the Struggle for the Temple Mount*. New York, London, Toronto, Sydney, Singapore: The Free Press. 2000.

GOTTWALD, NORMAN, K.: *The Politics of Ancient Israel*. Louisville, Kentucky: Westminster John Knox Press. 2001.

GRABBE, LESTER, L.: *Judaism from Cyrus to Hadrian. Volume One: The Persian and Greek Periods*. Minneapolis: Fortress Press, 1992.

GRABBE, LESTER, L.: *Ezra-Nehemiah*. London and New York: Routledge, 1998.

GRABBE, LESTER, L.: *Ancient Israel: What Do We Know and How Do We Know It?* U.S.A., T & T Clark, 2007.

GRAYZEL, SOLOMON: *A History of the Jews. From the Babylonian Exile to the Present: 5728-1968.* New York. A Mentor Book from New American Library. Times Mirror. 1968.

GRUEN, ERICH, S.: *Heritage and Hellenism: The Reinvention of Jewish Tradition*, University of California Press, Berkeley, Los Angeles, London, 1998, p. 335

HAIGH, REBEKAH: "Rebel Priests: The De Facto High Priesthood of the Early Maccabean Brothers," "Emory University," 2016. Permanent URL: https://etd.library.emory.edu/concern/etds/05741s38g?locale=d

HALBWACHS, MAURICE: *On Collective Memory*. Chicago and London. The University of Chicago Press. 1992.

HENRIQUES, JAMES CONNELL: "The Identity of the Hasideans of 1 and 2 Maccabees: A Re-Examination of the Topic with a Focus on the History of Scholarship," A Thesis Submitted to the Graduate Faculty of the University of Georgia in Partial Fulfillment of the Requirements for the Degree Master of Arts," Athens, Georgia, The University of Georgia, 2009.

HERZOG, CHAIM: *The Arab-Israeli Wars: War and Peace in the Middle East*. New York: Vintage Books. July 2005. 475 pages

INBARI, MOTTI: *Jewish Fundamentalism and the Temple Mount: Who Will Build the Third Temple?* New York. State University of New York. 2009.

JONAS, HANS: *The Gnostic Religion. The Message of the Alien God and the Beginnings of Christianity*. U.S., Beacon Press 1963 [1st. 1958].

JOSEPHUS, FLAVIUS: *The Works of Josephus. Complete and Unabridged* (William Whiston, A. M. translation)

KAMPEN, JOHN: *The Hasidean and the Origin of Pharisaism: A Study in 1 and 2 Maccabees*. Atlanta: Scholars Press. Society of Biblical Literature Septuagint and Cognate Studies Series. 1988

KESSLER, YOHANAN: "Persia's Loyal Yahwists: Power, Identity, and Ethnicity in Achaemenid Yehud," in *Judah and the Judeans in the Persian*

Period, ODED LIPSCHITS and MANFRED OEMING (eds.). Winona Lake, Indiana. Eisenbrauns. 2006

LIPSCHITS, ODED: ""Achaemenid Imperial Policy, Settlement Processes in Palestine, and the Status of Jerusalem in the Middle of the Fifth Century B.C.E.": Critical Notes on the Myth of the Mass Return," in *Judah and the Judeans in the Persian Period*, Oded Lipschits and Manfred Oeming (eds.). Winona Lake, Indiana. Eisenbrauns. 2006

LIVERANI, MARIO: *Israel's History and the History of Israel*. London, Oakville. Equinox. 2003/2005

MAZAR, BENJAMIN: "The Tobiads," "Israel Exploration Journal" 7. 1957.

MORRIS, BENNY: *1948: A History of the First Arab-Israeli War*. Yale University Press. 2008.

NEUSNER, JACOB: *Rabbinic Judaism: The Theological System*. Boston/Leiden. Brill. 2002.

NOTH, MARTIN: *The History of Israel*. New York and Evanston. Harper & Row, Publishers. 1960 [1958].

OLMSTEAD, A. T.: *History of the Persian Empire*. Chicago & London. Chicago University Press. 1948.

RABINOVICH, ABRAHAM: *The Yom Kippur War: The Epic Encounter that Transformed the Middle East*. New York. Schocken Books. 2004

ROWLEY, H. H.: *The Relevance of Apocalyptic*, Greenwood, S.C. 1944.

SACHAR, HOWARD, M.: *A History of Israel: From the Rise of Zionism to our Time*. New York: Alfred A. Knopf. 1976.

SAND, SHLOMO: *The Invention of the Jewish People.* London: New York. Verso. 2009.

SCHÄFER, PETER: "The Hellenistic and Maccabaean Periods," in HAYES, YOHANAN, H. and MILLER, MAXWELL, J. (eds.): *Israelite and Judaean History*. Philadelphia: The Westminster Press. 1977.

SCHNIEDEWIND, WILLIAM, M.: *How the Bible Became a Book: The Textualization of Ancient Israel*, Cambridge, New York, Cambridge University Press, 2004.

SCHNIEDEWIND, WILLIAM, M.: *Society and the Promise to David: The Reception History of 2 Samuel 7:1-17*, New York, Oxford University Press, 1999.

SCHWARTZ, DANIEL, R: "Antiochus IV Epiphanes in Jerusalem," Dept of Jewish History, Hebrew University, https://orion.huji.ac.il/symposiums/4th/papers/Schwartz99.html

SCHWARTZ, SET: *Imperialism and Jewish Society 200 BCE-640 CE*, Princeton; Oxford: Princeton University Press. 2001)

SHAPIRA, ANITA: *Israel: A History*. Waltham, Massachusetts. Brandeis University Press (translated from the Hebrew by Anthony Berris). 2012

SMITH, MORTON: *Palestinian Parties and Politics that Shaped the Old Testament*. New York and London, SCM Press Ltd. (2nd) 1987.

SPRINZAK, EHUD: The Ascendance of Israel's Radical Right. New York. Oxford University Press. 1991.

STERN, EPHRAIM: "The Religious Revolution in Persian-Period Judah," in *Judah and the Judeans in the Persian Period*, ODED LIPSCHITS and MANFRED OEMING (eds.). Winona Lake, Indiana. Eisenbrauns. 2006

TCHERIKOVER, VICTOR: *Hellenistic Civilization and the Jews*. Atheneum. New York, 1979. 563 pages.

VANDERHOOFT, DAVID STEPHEN: *The Neo-Babylonian Empire and Babylon in the Latter Prophets*. Scholars Press. Atlanta, Georgia, 1999.

VANDERKAM, JAMES, C.: *From Joshua to Caiaphas: High Priests After the Exile*. Minneapolis: Fortress Press, 2004.

WEINFELD, MOSHE: *Normative and Sectarian Judaism in the Second Temple Period*. London-New York. T & T Clark International. 2005.

WEINSTEIN, SARA EPSTEIN: *Piety and Fanaticism: Rabbinic Criticism of Religious Stringency*. Northvale, New Jersey. Jason Aronson Inc. 1997.

WIDENGREN, GEO: "The Persian Period," in HAYES, YOHANAN, H. and MILLER, MAXWELL, J. (eds.): *Israelite and Judaean History*. Philadelphia: The Westminster Press, 1977.

ZEITLIN, SOLOMON: *The Rise and Fall of the Judaean State*. Vol. One 332-337 B.C.E. Philadelphia. The Jewish Publication Society of America, 1968.